ALONE

Alone

A Widow's
Search for Joy

KATIE F. WIEBE

Tyndale House Publishers, Inc.
Wheaton, Illinois

Acknowledgment:
Portions of Chapter Ten, "When God Does Not Heal," appear in *Learning to Cope* by Helen Good Brenneman, and are reprinted by kind permission of Herald Press.

Library of Congress Catalog Card Number 76-275-72. ISBN: 0-8423-0062-7, paper. Copyright© 1976 by Tyndale House Publishers, Inc., Wheaton, Illinois. All rights reserved. Second printing, March 1977. Printed in the United States of America.

To Joanna, Susan,
Christine, and James

Contents

Part
One

CHAPTER ONE
The Beginning

There comes a time when one must decide about one's dreams—to risk everything to achieve them or to sit the rest of one's life in the backyard. —Anonymous*

"To be a widow is pure humiliation."

The speaker was a young widow with three small children. She spoke with certainty and yet without malice.

I stared at her unbelievingly. Surely she meant loneliness. I knew that the new life before me as a widow would be starkly empty of rich life relationships. Perhaps she meant difficulty?

A few weeks later when I was well into my novitiate as a widow, I began to understand what she'd meant. She had called it humiliation. The apostle James spoke of it as affliction. When the prophet Jeremiah wanted to describe the desolation of Jerusalem after the fall of Judah, he compared it to a widow: "How solitary lies the city, once so full of people! Once great among nations, now

*Tacked to Walter's bulletin board at his death.

become a widow" (Lamentations 1:1 NEB).

To me, the death of my husband Walter meant being ceremoniously ushered out of the life I'd known and enjoyed—albeit with music and processions and guests and feasting, all draped with the black crepe of sorrow —into a completely new way of living.

At first this new way seemed to be a continual stepping down and away from life, an emptying and a vast emptiness. A humiliation.

There was so little preparation for what has been the biggest, most difficult, and most challenging of life's tasks. Yet the beginning of this lonely experience moved only toward a tunnel in which the darkness became greater darkness.

It began in the fall of 1958. Our family, which included three children (Joanna, 11; Susan, 8; and Christine, 4) had just arrived in the Niagara Peninsula of Ontario. We had moved to eastern Canada from Saskatchewan after experiencing a dry, unpleasant summer in that prairie province where Walter and I had both spent many years. I was born there and grew up a child of cold northern Saskatchewan.

In the Canadian prairies, scorched grass struggled to remain alive in front yards. I couldn't call them lawns. Loose dust swirled about my every step and settled in the creases of shoes and clothes. In Ontario, everywhere we looked we saw green grass, the kind that could actually be mowed. Trees towered into the heavens instead of crouching to the earth like tired, worn-out old people. Brilliantly colored flowers nodded a welcome at every turn of the eye. Compared with the meager garden returns in Saskatchewan, the fruits and vegetables of the

Niagara Peninsula, the garden belt of Ontario, seemed like the first fruits of a new Eden. Further, by the time we arrived in early fall, the depressing humidity of the summer months had passed, and we were welcomed by wonderfully happy weather. If this was Ontario, we were going to love it and our new life here.

My husband Walter and I had come from a small pastorate in the prairies to teach in a private, church-related high school. Several years earlier in our marriage, after months of inner probing, we had committed ourselves to the cause of Christian journalism. Interest in this type of work was extremely limited in our small denomination. So was opportunity for it. Yet we felt God directing us, though we didn't know where the openings would eventually be. Now my husband planned to continue his education and eventually move into religious journalism. Before we moved, we had concluded that furthering his education would be possible in Ontario, at least on a part-time basis, with many universities within a radius of a hundred miles of the community where we planned to live. In the planning days of this adventure of moving to a new location, a new work, a new people, and with the hope of a new baby to be born in early winter, our enthusiasm pushed to Mount Everest levels.

At times I felt almost like my immigrant mother, who some thirty-five years earlier with husband and two small children, had left the threat of communist oppression, famine, and disease behind her in the Russian Ukraine for the hope of a new home and a new life in Canada. She and my father had never regretted their decision. So, as our family drove the long journey to Ontario, I could only repeat confidently to myself: *Prairies, with all your dust, small-town stodginess, next-year promises of better crops, though you have harbored and nurtured me for a lifetime, we are through with you. Ontario, here we come.*

And we came.

Finding a suitable house to rent while we decided where to locate permanently was difficult in an area congested with new immigrants. Many were refugees from Europe who had been sidetracked to Paraguay for a time until they could get entry permits to Canada. Finally the school board arranged for temporary quarters for our family in one of the school dormitories. The building, a two-story house with sloping veranda, dated back to the days of Colonel Ball and the War of 1812. The outside had long since lost its historical appeal and looked more like Grandmother's gown made over for granddaughter. The old brick had been sheathed with stucco and the trim updated with paint. Once inside, however, it took little imagination to envision gracious ladies with powdered hair piled high, trailing their hoop skirts down the large open staircase or relaxing with their gentlemen before the generous fireplace in the parlor to discuss the inclement weather. But that vision vanished rapidly when high school girls in white blouses and navy-blue jumpers, undergirded by layers of frothy crinolines, (this was the fifties) rushed up and down the stairs in white bobby socks and saddle shoes to classes and other activities.

The rooms we were to live in were scattered over two floors. Some of the students lived next door to our two roomy bedrooms. The one my husband and I occupied measured more than twenty-four feet in length and about eight feet in width. A large bay window bulged out of the front wall. In a pinch the room could be used as a race track, I concluded, when I first saw it, thinking about the small house we'd left behind. The children bounced around in a bedroom at least eighteen feet by eighteen. Kitchen and living room had been improvised in what was formerly the dining room of the colonial family.

We moved into this helter-skelter kind of arrangement, assuring ourselves it was only temporary. As soon as possible we would look for something better. So we patiently shared bathroom privileges with teen-agers who seemed to think the bathroom was society's most recent invention. I mopped endless lengths of painted wooden floors to trap the giant dustballs. I struggled with an elementary kitchen plumbing system that led into an open tub in the basement. Periodically I had to send a child down to check whether it was ready for emptying. At times when the dampness of the Ontario winter seeped through the ancient walls, I was sure the heating system had also originated in the War of 1812. Yet these were minor inconveniences. We were sure God had great things in store for us.

The first week of teaching in the private high school was disappointing for Walter. Adjustment to a new school system and to new fellow-workers and students, friendly as they were, wasn't easy. His health, which had been a minor problem for several weeks, suddenly became a major concern. Just before we left Saskatchewan, the children had had severe cases of stomach flu. On the trip to Ontario, Walter had experienced the same kind of abdominal pain and nausea. Now his illness returned. The first weekend he lay in bed, doubled up with pain.

The doctor could find no immediate cause for his sickness. The pain in his abdomen subsided the next day, but the general malaise continued week after week. Each new day in the Promised Land became an exquisite kind of torture without any apparent medical help. Walter's "flu" hung on week after week, month after month. He dragged himself to school in the morning, so unlike his usual self. He had always been the one to leap into the day with energy and joy, pulling me out after an extra twenty minutes in the warm bed.

The dismally cold, damp weather affected us all, accustomed as we were to a dry, though more severe, cold in the prairies. Nights were punctuated by hacking coughs, days by continuous wiping of noses. The light of God's promise to us, so clear when we left Saskatchewan, grew darker each day, especially the morning in the eighth month of my pregnancy when I tripped on the beautiful open staircase and sprained my ankle. That accident seemed to be the last bitter pill to swallow as I hobbled and bobbled around the vast expanse of our living quarters. I wanted desperately to go back to old friends, old ways of living, old securities, and to a God who didn't force us through enigmatic experiences.

But somehow life doesn't stop for sprained ankles, pregnancy, respiratory problems, days of freezing rain, or a sick and depressed husband. On November 23 when our son James Philip was born, a ray of happiness beamed into what seemed to be a first-class fiasco. From the beginning we called him *Frintel Wieb*, a Low German expression of endearment meaning Happy Wiebe, because of his pleasant, placid disposition. We loved and enjoyed this innocent newcomer, despite the unhappy environment into which he had come.

With the help of antibiotics and other medication, Walter had been able to keep up with his duties, although without much enthusiasm. When the request came to attend a church publications board meeting at Hillsboro, Kansas, some 1,500 miles away, between Christmas and New Year's, I encouraged him to go if he felt strong enough. I secretly hoped that a break from the routine and the sight of old friends might help him get over whatever was bothering his system and give him new inspiration. Maybe the doctor was right when he said it was a nervous condition. Armed with a new supply of pills, he left for Winnipeg immediately after Christmas, planning to continue on to Hillsboro. I dug in for a week alone with the children, the weather, and Colonel Ball's ancient house.

One morning as I was mopping our private race track, the sun streamed through the window, burning the specks of dust into gleaming gold. I stood and watched. The silent beauty of the moment lifted my spirit. I thought to myself: *Maybe now after Christmas our circumstances will improve.*

And almost as swiftly, like a definite response to my inner thoughts, the words came to me: *No, deeper still.* I pushed the mop hurriedly over the floor, almost startled by the experience. Not one to accept supernatural phenomena readily, I found this inner experience too real to be disregarded, yet too unreal to be shared with anyone. A voice? Nonsense. I continued my work.

Later that evening a phone call from a friend in Hillsboro reported that Walter had collapsed at one of the board meetings. The doctors had advised hospitalization.

The diagnosis was not yet definite, but they would keep me informed. Walter's poor health of the fall months had finally climaxed.

Perhaps only years later does one realize the perplexities such moments create. What should I do? I tried to sort out my thoughts. The children were naturally disappointed that Walter wouldn't be coming home for New Year as planned, but took it quite well. They were also fairly well physically, although Joanna still coughed if she got too much cold air or overexerted herself. Jamie's cold had been severe, but he was getting better. Chrissie had been feverish, but her temperature had come down. Susan had been throwing up, but was also improving. I had had a cold, but was now in the mopping-up stages. I considered going to Hillsboro to see Walter.

New Year's Day I was downstairs alone in our combination kitchen/dining/living room before anyone else, pondering the whole situation, when the words, "This is the will of God concerning you," forced themselves into my mind. I couldn't rid myself of these words. The will of God. Hadn't we put God's will for our lives at the top of our list of priorities? I tried to remember what the rest of the verse was, so at the first free moment I paged through the epistles, looking for phrases that looked familiar. Then I found it. "In everything give thanks: for this is the will of God . . . concerning you" (1 Thessalonians 5:18).

Give thanks for this? A sick husband, unsatisfactory living conditions, unhappy children, rainy and sloppy weather? I felt as if someone had slapped me in the face. All I wanted was to find a spot of sanity in this supermess. But the word was "everything." Somewhere in this chaos God expected me to find something to be thankful for. At the moment I couldn't, but I determined at least to remember the verse.

On January 5, 1959, I received a telegram stating that Walter had been operated on that morning. The operation was serious, revealing a ruptured appendix, badly infected. The doctors believed he would survive. The pieces fell into place. The first attack had occurred on the trip to Ontario in early September. He had walked around all fall with a ruptured appendix.

I read and reread the telegram, trying to glean additional information from its few words. What should I do? My first concern was for Walter's healing, my second that I might go to him. The third was for the children and their needs while I was gone.

The traditional Prayer Week of the New Year had just begun in the churches in the vicinity. A few phone calls brought promises of prayer for Walter's health from places as far away as Saskatchewan and Alberta, as well as Ontario. A telephone call to my mother in Saskatchewan to ask her to care for the children brought the response, "I'll be there in the morning." Grandma willingly agreed to look after the three older girls. Little Jamie, small in size but big in needs, was too much for her to handle, so I continued to pray before her arrival that God might send me someone to look after him so I could leave.

That afternoon as I continued my preparations to travel to Kansas by train, a young woman carrying a basket of apples knocked on the door. I recognized her immediately as my fellow patient in the hospital at the time Jamie was born. While we, as a family, had rejoiced at the birth of our son, she and her husband had grieved over the death of their premature baby. I noted how this young couple often found comfort and strength in Bible reading and prayer. Yet she went home from the hospital empty-handed, and I had brought home our promise of joy.

This friendly person standing at my door wanted to know what she could do to help me. I knew immediately that God had sent her to me. I briefly explained my need.

"I'm just the person," she responded. "I have nothing to do most of the day. I'm feeling well, and I'd love to take care of your baby."

My heart went out to this young woman, who, though she had lost her own child, was willing to care for mine. How wonderfully God caused "all things to work together for good." God had provided for my immediate needs and I could go to Walter.

Grandma Funk arrived the next morning. The children were overjoyed. The difficult experiences of watching their father slowly wither before their eyes had begun to affect their spirits, and now Grandma's coming offset that misery the moment she stepped in the door. Placid Chrissie was so excited at seeing Grandma of the happy days, she became unmanageable. Joanna and Susan could hardly believe their eyes.

I left for Hillsboro and remained there with Walter about a week. I returned assured and thankful that his recovery was certain. We praised God.

Approximately three weeks later, Walter flew to Ontario, only to have a sudden relapse and be required to spend another ten days in the local hospital. Those who have been through similar experiences will recognize the thoughts that return to tempt one that God has finally deserted his children. He doesn't care after all. I tried to keep up with the mundane things of life—such as cooking, cleaning, diapering—while my body and spirit shouted that life was too hard. How could anyone find something in this mixed-up state of affairs to be thankful for?

I think Walter felt the same way at times, yet a spirit of submission to the will of God shone through his letters to the children during this second stay in the hospital. He wrote to the girls: "After breakfast I brush my teeth and then rest awhile and take time to read the Bible and pray. I pray for Mama and you girls and Jamie. I pray that God will give me health, and I pray that he will help me here to be a witness for him."

His convalescence was slow because of the lengthy period the infection had preyed on his system. Little did we know at the time that we had begun the first of a series of operations in a fight for his physical life, and an even stiffer battle for spiritual survival. I often felt like a person ordered to cross a bottomless chasm. My dark abyss of doubt and despair could only be vaulted by the leap of faith, but I wanted a solid crosswalk.

We came through that winter with few high moments. After several months, toward spring, when Walter was able to return to teaching, we started to think again of long-range plans to move into religious journalism. Like a child quieted after a long period of heavy sobbing, we began to move back into a regular routine. We were still in Colonel Ball's ancient dwelling. The weather was still wet and sleety. The children hadn't yet adjusted to Ontario ways, but Walter was getting better and we were all a year older.

In early fall Walter wrote in his journal: "A year has

passed by since our coming to Ontario. A great sense of this swiftly passing life has come over me during this year. It seems that so many years have been eaten by the locust . . . cankerworm . . . caterpillar . . . palmer worm. What are these insects that eat away our lives and jeopardize fruition? Has it been indolence, sloth, lack of perseverance, failing to continually press toward the mark? . . . God, forgive me."

CHAPTER TWO
In Kindergarten

Between the great things we cannot do and the small things we will not do, the danger is that we shall do nothing. —Monod

In the fall of 1959 we moved to Kitchener, Ontario, a city of about 70,000 at the time, with a university in the twin city of Waterloo. Walter had accepted a teaching position in our denominational Bible school, hoping that the smaller school situation would be less taxing on his health and would also give him time to finish his studies toward the bachelor of arts degree. As he taught and studied, I turned to free-lance writing. Before long, two busy but pleasant winters had passed.

In our second spring in Kitchener, when Walter took a routine physical examination for graduate school entrance, the doctor discovered a growth in his lower abdomen. He checked into the matter, had X-rays taken, but even these didn't reveal the true nature of the problem. After consultation with another doctor, we finally agreed to have surgery done on May 30. Because Walter seemed in generally good health and his weight stable, the delay seemed justified. The doctor wasn't unduly concerned.

The day Walter was to be admitted to the hospital for exploratory surgery, he left our house by street car. As yet I didn't have a driver's license, a continuing source of frustration to me. I wanted him to take a taxi, but he figured that taxis were a luxury he could do without as long as he was healthy. What were his feelings as he left, having already spent so much time in a hospital? I don't know. I could see only the gigantic mountain that had moved back into its place before us, and I felt too numb to start climbing.

Why did we have to go through this experience again? Hadn't we had our share of discomfort and pain? And as usual, the sickness of one member of the family brought along with it a host of other problems to make life even more complicated. One was my inability to drive, a skill never encouraged for women in the small rural communities of Saskatchewan where a person could walk from one end of town to the other in three minutes. I had taken lessons from a commercial driving school, but failed my first attempt to pass the test. I, a grown woman, who considered myself fairly capable and responsible, couldn't even learn to drive a car. I came home to weep and rail against the heartless examiner. Without a license to drive, it was difficult to get the children to their various appointments and destinations, and even to visit Walter at the hospital. A trip to see him was a complicated procedure by public transportation, transferring from one bus to another, taking a great deal of time and energy. I couldn't say thanks to God for this—the daily frustration of finding babysitters, missing buses, trying to be cheerful, wondering where the money would come from this time.

The operation brought a more serious cause for concern. The surgeons who first saw the three- to four-pound mucous cyst they had removed from Walter's abdomen feared the worst—that it was malignant. But even the most experienced doctor among them was unable to diagnose it immediately; he had never seen anything like it in his long practice. The pathologist called upon other help in Toronto in the search for an accurate diagnosis. Days of anxious waiting followed. Walter was seriously ill the first three days, yet I had the family to care for. He wanted me with him; the children needed me at home.

Finally the good news came from the doctor that a diagnosis had been made. The tumor was not malignant, but there was a danger of recurrence. The doctors thought that the root cause was the ruptured appendix of several years before, so another operation was scheduled to remove the stub of the appendix later that summer. Before the next operation Walter wrote in his journal, " We rest on God's Word: 'When thou passest through the waters, I will be with thee . . . Fear not: for I am with thee' " (Isaiah 43:1-5).

I believe we were thankful in that waiting period. One tries hard to be grateful for all signs that life will go on. We praised God for this word from the medical profession. To us it was a signal to live and not to die. Only those who live with chronic illness can know how one sick member can bring the life of an entire family to a halt. Outings, visits, trips must all be eliminated while energy is poured into keeping up the health and spirits of the sick person. As Walter's health returned, we tried to bring a semblance of hope and joy to the family. We went camping into Algon-quin Park in northern Ontario to enjoy the haunting shriek of loons and the grumpy croak of bullfrogs. About fifteen years later some of the children made a return pilgrimage to this spot which for a brief moment seemed idyllic and tranquil at a time when our circumstances resembled the aftermath of a Kansas tornado.

Later that summer the third operation was performed. Once again we believed that the matter of Walter's physical condition had been settled. The appendix stub was out. Surely his illness had finally been arrested. Yet it would be wrong not to admit that at times the weakness of despair pierced through the overriding current of faith and hope. We were tired of sickness. We longed for health. I felt like a sheet on the line on a windy day, twisted and battered.

Walter wrote in his journal: " 'Be thou exalted' (Psalm 57:5). God wants to be exalted in and through our lives. This is what he is striving for through the experiences of life. There is divine purpose. We are to decrease, but he shall increase. How much shall we decrease? To which point? To the point of extinction? Not the extinction of self, that is, our individuality, for God does not wish to destroy us. But of selfish interest, ambition, desire . . . When many of these things are so much a part of us, the experience of being loosed from them is a painful and crushing experience. O God, how much more must you crush us?

"The deepest experiences of the soul in these things are most difficult to communicate to others—to explain to others and to share with them what one has felt and thought and feared, and what a struggle it has been to maintain faith and hope and courage. But be thou exalted, O Lord. It is your right . . . but, Lord, I need your strength to sustain me. I am a poor, weak creature—but a product of your Creator-hand."

Walter was accepted in the fall of 1961 by New York's Syracuse University in the religious journalism sequence of a master's program. The decision made on our knees nearly thirteen years earlier in a little country school-house on the prairies of Saskatchewan was coming to ful-fillment. In Syracuse, Walter lived in an apartment with a Nigerian and a Formosan, both also attending the uni-versity. They called it their little League of Nations. I remained behind in Kitchener with the children. It seemed too much to ask the children to move again so soon for a temporary reason.

The winter promised to be long and rugged for us, as our finances by now were nearly depleted. I felt as if we were walking on thin ice, but as long as we kept moving, we might stay on top and not sink through to the bottom. I planned to work part-time at various office jobs, at baby-sitting, and at some free-lance writing, in addition to taking care of the children and helping Walter with re-search for his courses.

Some people are critical of families who break apart temporarily for reasons such as ours or even for mission-ary or church-related service. I have no answer to their criticism except we felt that God was asking this decision of us. He had given his word as a bond, "I will never leave thee, nor forsake thee" (Hebrews 13:5). Surely this was better than stocks and bonds or money in the bank? Yet before the long winter had even begun, I was haunted by apprehension. Would his grace be sufficient for some-thing as difficult as our situation? A husband in precarious health, limited finances, four children—with the oldest moving into a troubled adolescence and the youngest still in diapers. Again and again I was drawn to that passage to read the rest of it: "So that we may boldly say, The Lord is my helper, and I will not fear what man shall do unto me."

Before we had finished saying goodbye to Daddy at the bus stop, our first mistake was apparent. Two-year-old Jamie shrieked, "Bad Daddy, I hate you." His explosion was so sudden and unexpected, I couldn't imagine what was wrong.

Little son, we hadn't told you Daddy would be going away alone. You expected to board the bus with him and go to Grandma's. You weren't ready to say goodbye.

I didn't know then that that winter would be my kindergarten lesson in living alone. In another year that experience would be mine as a widow. Before that time I had many lessons to learn in patience, prayer, and trust. I was truly a kindergartner, and a frightened one at that.

That first evening after the children had gone to bed, after the doors had been securely locked and checked twice, I sat alone at my husband's empty desk at which I still often work. The months of living alone that now faced me suddenly became several eternities. Into the shadows slipped an enemy who was to become a familiar companion later on. Mockingly he suggested, "Now isn't it too bad that you have to be here alone, while your friends have husbands to keep them company? Did God actually ask you to bring your family up by yourself? Isn't this a little ridiculous?"

I could recognize my enemy from previous acquaintance. His name is Self-pity. I knew that if I gave him even a brief nod, he would call in a host of his cohorts: loneliness, discouragement, fear, worry, and envy of anyone whose life was tranquil and undisturbed.

That first evening I had no husband's firm hand to encourage me, no husband's shoulder to weep on. I had only God's Word, which was to be my resource for inner strength throughout that winter when strength and wisdom were depleted. I knew that my own spiritual temperature would determine the climate of our home life. My relationship to Christ was not a thing I could take for granted. It would be dependent on the nurture it received in my own experience.

The winter was to be an adventure with God to see how he would meet our needs as he had promised. Though I was circumscribed in what I was able to do outside the home because of the needs of the children, I learned that our four brick walls weren't a prison to shut me in. My spirit was free to wander with the great saints of God and other writers. It was a winter dedicated to much reading and studying.

Well-meaning friends, who knew our plans for the winter, and were aware of how lonesome life might become, advised me, "Get out and see people so the time won't drag." "Find some exhausting work." "Occupy your mind." They added kind words and looks of sympathy. If I agreeably added my own sympathy to theirs, by nightfall I was in a sea of tears. One missionary's wife told me, "Throughout the years of long absences from my husband, I have realized that I must never pity myself." Friends asked, "Don't you get afraid at night?" If I did, sentimental sighing over the situation never helped. I found it best to stay away from the chronic sympathizers.

We wrote many letters that winter, for Walter came home only at longer vacations such as Thanksgiving, Christmas, Easter, and spring break. We wrote about dreams and hopes, about sorrows and frustrations, about ten-cent kites and $2,000 loans, about jokes and gripes.

Walter: "This winter we have prayed more for each other, perhaps, than ever before. The Lord has great and good purposes for us, in the way in which he leads us. It certainly has given us new insights and understandings, which we would not readily have received without this way."

Katie: "Jamie chuckled all over when I read him your letter. Chrissie is your big letter enthusiast. She loves to write replies with almost a fanatical zeal. Her problem is tenses—if she writes 'tomorrow' and if you get it tomorrow, how will you know which day the event took place?"

Walter: "Yes, children, I bought a kite—two of them, one paper and one plastic—at the reduced price of 10 cents each at the corner drugstore. I don't know when we'll have a chance to fly them. I'll bring them when I come home."

Katie: "I sometimes think that if you hadn't gone away, I would never have learned to drive the car as well as I do. It was something like being pushed off the deep end of a wharf. It's a great temptation to worry about you and your health, especially since people always ask about it. But then I know I can do nothing about it anyway, so I trust the Lord to look after you—and he is, I know. Don't get too lonesome. These last weeks before you come will be the worst because of the actual waiting. I get lonely too—here in the evenings by myself—wondering, waiting, hoping."

Walter: "Well, this is the day for me here. We got back our outlines of the biography today. Dave and I got *A*'s. All the others were in the *B* range. Boy, were Dave and I thrilled. To get one *A* from Wolseley—boy, what an accomplishment . . . I have been feeling fine. The scale here says l93. Figure that out."

Katie: "How good God is to us. I have been trying so far to take care of groceries and incidentals out of money I earn. This morning I was out of money for the first time; I had only about 25 cents left, and I haven't been able to earn anything, so I committed it to God last night. If nothing turned up, I was simply going to write a check on our savings account for some money. This evening when Mrs. Klassen came to pick up Joanna for a baby-sitting job, she gave me an envelope with $10. It was really overwhelming. It will tide me over until my baby check [government family allowance] comes at the end of the week. This winter has been quite an adventure in faith that God will provide."

Walter: "Jamie, you went out 'chrick and chreating'? Was it fun? Did you get a lot of candy? Will you give me a piece when I come home? Or did you eat it all? Shall I bring you some candy? When I come home I will read you a story. Chrissie, does somebody help you at the table with your grapefruit like I always did? Or do you do it alone now?"

Katie: "Yesterday afternoon we all went skating. Even your dear wife entrusted her aging bones to the uncertainties of skates . . . at least today they feel aging. The children thought it was simply wonderful. There was quite a group from the church, and we had borrowed skates for Susan, so they all had fun, even Jamie, just running around like a headless chicken."

Walter: "My thoughts go to each one of you: Joanna, so much of your life hidden at Eastwood Collegiate; Susan, struggling sometimes with midweek lessons; Chrissie, wanting to sit beside Daddy; Jamie, wanting to have Daddy read a story; Mother, Daddy would like to love her!"

Surgeons now use a type of deep-freeze anesthetic in long and difficult operations. At times that winter I wished for the same treatment. I envied the animals who hibernate in winter. Yet I knew God held me responsible for the life I lived while we were apart. I couldn't live on past memories nor could I live only in anticipation of Walter's return. *When Walter comes home, we will clean the basement. When Daddy comes back, we will visit the zoo.* Life had to be lived now.

That winter I learned what problems I would face a year later as a widow. Each married couple gathers its own little store of patterns of living over the years. The early riser turns up the thermostat, the last one to bed locks the door. The husband is responsible for keeping the car in good repair. Mother looks after grocery shopping and meals. In the evening, time is set aside for tea and talk and prayer before bed. Separation, even if only temporary, requires a complete rearrangement of living style. Where I formerly leaned heavily on Walter for making decisions, I alone had to decide when the car needed an oil change. I was the highest court of appeal when the children had arguments. I was both the best liked and most hated parent at all times.

In Kindergarten

After Walter left, I soon noticed that as a manless woman I had no easy social interaction. Married circles lay down certain social laws: two people can always be accommodated at nearly any kind of function, if need be, but one alone is a strain. I found that I was often an odd one at social functions—someone left over after pairs were made—to be classified with the widows and single women. And because of this I found many new friends I otherwise would never have known. Being strained through this social sieve turned up gems I never knew existed.

The children, however, couldn't always understand why Daddy had to be away. "I wish my daddy would come home," Jamie sobbed. And I wished it too. One night Jamie prayed his usual evening prayer, "And keep me safe till morning light." Then he hesitated before he said, "And keep this Jamie [pointing to himself] safe, and keep Daddy safe." Inwardly I was also pointing to myself, "And keep this Mama from getting too discouraged."

Again and again I had to explain that Daddy was away because he wanted to learn to serve God better. Yet little children grow hungry for father-love, and cannot understand such ideal ambitions. Our little boy turned to a snapshot Walter had sent home to us and with the dawning of recognition shouted exultantly, "We got one of those Daddies too."

As I think back to that winter, I can remember many times when the situation finally seemed impossible. I was tired and cross because the money had run out, the toddler had turned the refrigerator control to its coldest and the milk had frozen, spilling onto the shelves. Forgetting that I planned to pick her up after school, Joanna had come home by bus while I sat outside the school and fumed. The driveway had to be shoveled clear of snow for the third time in one week. The children became unruly. The nights seemed endless, and the days never long enough. I ached with loneliness. I wondered at times if the Lord really had a place for us. Did we fit in anywhere? Why had we ever started on such a harebrained venture?

I found that reading Christian biographies was one of the greatest helps in my own times of perplexity. One of many books I read that winter was Isobel Kuhn's *Greenleaf in Drought-time*, the account of the experiences of two China Inland Mission workers while under house arrest by the communists. They had given away all their possessions except the barest essentials because they had expected to leave China within a few days. For two years they lived in a stripped-down life style with only Christ as their companion. The book showed me clearly that Christians who seek spiritual help must not attribute the circumstances of their lives to "second causes." Instead, we should accept everything that moves into our lives as something that God has permitted. Evil agents have no sovereignty of their own. The evil, the affliction in life, happens only because God allows it. Christians have only God to contend with, none other. There can never be any blaming, wondering why, or rationalizing of the events of our life. Our focus should only be our relationship with Christ. I couldn't blame anyone—neither negligent doctors, unfortunate circumstances, nor difficult relationships; I couldn't wonder why our lives weren't smooth-flowing like those of friends; I couldn't ask why we were poor and others rich.

As winter wore into spring, new doubts came in the form of a recurrence of Walter's illness. The doctors had said it might recur, but so soon? Little Jamie, in his child-like way, seemed always able to fashion the words better than I could. One day he had to stay in the house because of an attack of croup the night before. "I sad" was his way of expressing his feelings when he didn't feel particularly well. The recurring symptoms of Walter's illness made us all sad. And frightened. But we couldn't stop living.

At the close of the school term as we began to plan for the following year, Walter was once again in the hospital with an intestinal infection. After a thorough examina-tion, the doctors decided that neither further medication nor surgery would help at that time. The best procedure would be to return home, watch his diet carefully, and learn to live with his condition. Again, the doctors seemed certain his illness wasn't a malignancy but a type of pseudocancer that originated from the irritation of the long-infected appendix.

In the hospital Walter wrote: "I asked the Lord for a word today, and I came upon Psalm 139. First of all, there are the great truths of God's omniscience and omnipres-ence. These are very precious and comforting truths for the child of God, for the one who is at peace with God through Jesus Christ. Then it is wonderful to know that he knows all about me and also, no matter where he leads me, lo, he is there! The psalmist concludes, however, with a serious prayer: 'Search me, O God, and know my heart: try me and know my thoughts: and see if there be any wicked way in me, and lead me in the way everlasting.' It is my prayer this morning, too. It is a wholesome prayer: see if there be any wicked way in me, cleanse me from it completely, and I will be led in the way everlasting."

The next weeks were some of the longest and most difficult we had faced as yet. We debated with ourselves, with the doctors, and with God: which way should we go? How quickly would the illness progress? Should Walter return to school the following winter to complete his work toward a master's degree in religious journalism? Should he accept a position in a publishing house? Should we just wait for him to die?

We were tempted to come before God and say to him as Martha had, "Lord, if you had been here, Lazarus would not have died" (John 11). Lord, if you had been around, all this sickness would never have happened, and we could be faithfully serving you now in some work. But as the Lord countered Martha's "if" with his own *if,* so he met us with the words, "If you believe . . ." The glory of God could come out of our "if" if we believed and made a power out of it for God.

Walter's condition was medically rare, and the prognosis indefinite. So we proceeded with our earlier plans to move to Hillsboro, Kansas, where Walter was planning to take the position of book editor of our denominational publishing house. To wait for death was to die by slow torture. To do nothing was to rot. We had hazarded our "all" in this venture of doing what we thought God wanted us to do. As Walter wrote in his journal: "If God really wants us there in Hillsboro in that work, he will get us there. We believe he wants us there, but we have found out that if the Lord wants us to go ahead, he doesn't necessarily promise that the road ahead will be smooth blacktop." It wasn't.

Visas, health certificates, medical insurance. Everything worked out well to emigrate to the United States. The road was rutty, but at least gravel-topped for a time. In September 1962 the moving van loaded up our early-attic and late-basement furniture. We piled into our 1953 rust-colored Chevrolet and headed for Kansas. "We should not stop trying to do something as long as the Lord gives strength," Walter wrote.

Walter began his work, and the children enrolled in Hillsboro schools. I accepted a part-time job as book-keeper in an office. Hillsboro was lauded as the "Land of Milk and Honey" on the billboards leading into the city because of its large milk-producing plant and honey factory. The children agreed. A cold storage locker plant butchered pigs and sold products such as cracklings and smoked sausage to their many customers. We found a place to buy milk, cream, and eggs cheaply. We could again enjoy the luxury of topping desserts with whipped cream, a delicacy we had left far behind in rural Saskatchewan. The girls decided they wouldn't go back to Ontario for anything.

We also began to know the people of the community and their churches. We wanted God to be the ground-stuff of our lives, yet in this strange country we felt our own darkness, and we reached out our hands timidly toward the hand of God.

After about seven weeks in Walter's new job, health again became an issue. The doctors no longer knew what to do. Our only resort was God, so we prayed a great deal and friends prayed with us. Not as a desperate measure, but in obedience to God's Word, we called the elders of the church to anoint him with oil and to pray over him. He seemed a little better after that.

A few days later on a Thursday evening he called me from the office to say he felt sick. That evening I took him to the hospital. The memory I cherish most even today is the sight of him drawing our three-year-old son gently to him and murmuring, "My little boy." At our last family devotion, as he lay on the living room couch, we sang "As we walk with the Lord in the light of his Word, what a glory he sheds on our way." Was this the way of glory? How haggard, how tired he looked.

On Sunday morning, with great hesitancy, the doctor told me he thought Walter's life on earth might end at any time. Another mucous tumor was growing rapidly in his abdomen and constricting his internal organs. The medical profession had done what it could.

I began calling relatives. His mother, his brothers and sisters, my parents, my sisters and brother, friends, the churches we had left behind. And one by one old friends and new ones came to sit by his bedside or to take care of the children while I spent most of my time in the hospital.

Joanna, my oldest daughter, told me later how she had clung to the fact that Daddy had just bought himself a new pair of black shoes the week before, so he couldn't die. He had to wear the shoes. It seemed clear that in spite of God's sustaining grace for so many years, his grace would now have to be sufficient in other ways. One day as I sat beside my husband and looked at his sunken cheeks, his swollen fevered lips, his struggle for breath, I told God he should take Walter to himself. I could let him go.

As Walter hovered in that in-between land of consciousness and coma, he turned to me one day to ask, "It seems all golden before me. What shall I do?" I encouraged him to move toward the land which seemed so bright to him and where there would be no pain, no sickness, no sorrow. In the few clear moments he had toward the last he himself commented that it was "better to be with the Lord."

The following Saturday, early in the morning, Walter slipped quietly into the land from which there is no recall. As the sounds of death rattled in his throat, I called the nurse and Walter's sister Susie, who had been with me for the last few days. In a few moments it was over. Four years of struggling between illness and health ended in this little hospital room in Hillsboro. The nurse gently closed his eyes and slipped his dentures into his mouth, covered him, and guided me out. Walter was dead. I was a widow. My children were fatherless.

I walked out of the hospital to tell the children that the long struggle was over. I knew that the trust God had given me through weeks of difficult living remained with me—not as a strong, blinding light, but as a tiny glimmer of hope in the gathering darkness. I would now get a chance to use my kindergarten lessons of the previous year.

CHAPTER THREE

The Affliction

The handles of my plow with tears are wet, the shears with rust are spoiled; and yet, and yet, my God, my God, keep me from turning back.—Anonymous

When a person dies, particularly if that person is a young father or mother, the community and church stands aghast at the monstrous deed which God has permitted. How could he, they mutter under their soul's breath. Quickly friends and loves ones rally around the bereaved persons and bear them up in prayer and with other kinds of support. They visit, bring food, babysit, help with the housework. Such help is a great source of strength and comfort during the first weeks of sorrow when numerous decisions and adjustments must be made.

But life doesn't stand still because someone has died. Friends and relatives must return to their own responsibilities. Gradually the strong undergirding of prayer, the visits, the words of comfort, the letters and the cards thin out.

One day, usually a dull day when everything has gone

wrong—the washing machine has broken down, the bank has issued a statement that the account is overdrawn, one of the children has come home with a rip in his new jacket—the widow realizes she is now alone. Her husband isn't there. She can't run home to Mama. Friends can be expected to help out only so long. And then she happens to overhear that some of her old friends are going to a Chinese restaurant tonight and have left her out of the party.

What word conveys the image of destitution and loneliness as surely as the word *widow*?

"I just hate that word," said one woman who had lost her husband. "I wish there were another word that could be used."

In nineteenth century literature, writers or speakers who wished to depict a character who had the whole world pitted against him chose a widow's son. In Bible times, widows knew real affliction. Frequently they were left without financial support or even the opportunity to earn a living. Without a spokesman of any kind, they became the prey of ruthless moneylenders. The plight of widows even now in underprivileged countries is dismal; their marital state pushes them to the bottom of the social and economic ladder.

Widows in our country aren't usually faced with starvation as a class. Their affliction takes on a different pattern, strongly influenced by the prevailing attitudes of society toward women and the limitations placed upon their contribution. The affliction is primarily psychological. They are persons without portfolios. "You suddenly feel as if the train has kept going, but the car you were on has been shunted onto a siding," one widow said.

Walter died on November 17, 1962, so our first Christmas in the new community contained a strange mixture of joy over the birth of Christ and grief over the death of a husband and father. The people of the community, who were very ready to help, accented my new role as a widow in a strange way. One evening, shortly before Christmas, a deacon from one of the local churches stood at the door with a 25-pound sack of flour on his shoulder, a gift from the church.

Now I am a widow, I thought to myself. The typical poor widow of every old novel I've ever read. Now people bring me flour and castoff clothing. Perhaps I'll be expected to take in washing and scrub floors to support my four fatherless children. I've often wondered since whether the man sensed my bewilderment at his gift and how it frightened me. It seemed to be pushing me into a role I didn't want. He was telling me, "You are a widow." I was saying loudly within myself, "I am not—not yet, not yet!"

Death begins a chain of activities intertwined with a chain of emotions from which it is impossible to wrench oneself. These two processes move along together, often not quite in agreement, but holding the widow prisoner with their double strength. At the funeral when people expect a show of grief, the widow may display no outward emotion. She moves through the funeral dry-eyed and strong. On another lighter occasion, she may suddenly burst into tears for no apparent reason, making her friends wonder why she can't control herself better after so many weeks.

Immediately after a death, relatives must be notified. Funeral arrangements must be made. The obituary must be written. Plans must be considered for what will happen after the funeral. I moved into this activity in a state of shock while another person in me went through the visible motions of making arrangements, talking to the children, arranging for housing for the relatives who began arriving almost immediately, answering the door-bell to acknowledge visitors and their kind gifts of food.

When I began the funeral arrangements with the local pastor, I thought to myself that this would probably be a very small funeral. I almost pitied myself and the chil-dren. We five and a few relatives to bury Walter! What a send-off for one who had lived so faithfully! On the day of the funeral, a cold snowy day in November, the church was almost filled with friends from the community, the children's schoolmates, and all Walter's brothers and sisters except one, as well as his mother. It was almost like a family reunion. The service was held in the morning, followed by a luncheon provided by the women of the church.

My sister Frieda remained with me for the first few days, guiding me through the maze of activities that had to be taken care of. Though I had lived with Walter's ill-ness for several years, steeling myself for the eventuality of death, when it came, I found myself as unprepared as a passenger in a boat who is suddenly dumped in the water. I realize now that this state of blank bewilderment is fairly normal for anyone moving through the grief process. Arranging for the funeral, making immediate financial arrangements, seeing a lawyer, procuring death certificates—the sight of which almost sickens one after awhile, for every legal document requires at least

one copy—all added to the burden. Frieda was a wonderful help.

There were letters to write. Cards. Notes of acknowledgment. Frieda, as my temporary secretary, made lists
for me of what I had to do. I wrote letter after letter at
her suggestion to friends who wanted to know the details
of Walter's death and our plans for the future. Now as I
reread the carbon copies of these letters, I find the image
of a woman who was calm, possessed, in control. I don't
see the woman who walked through days and weeks with
a cold, hard lump inside, determined mainly to get
through each day, almost hoping the next one wouldn't
come.

Every morning when I awoke I faced a new batch of
tasks to look after, some of which I knew something
about, others totally new. The brakes of the car needed
repair, one of the children needed new shoes, another
six letters had to be written, the landlord had to be reminded of the leaking faucet. Inside I had little or no feeling, except for general nausea at the sight of food and
the overwhelming sensation, "This can't go on. My
circumstances have finally become too much for God
and for me." I was far removed from relatives on both
sides of the family, and when Frieda finally had to return
to her family, I still felt like an unoiled machine moving
through the motions of living. Each motion was a strain.

If at first I felt shock, I think the next stage in my
emotional development was a feeling of fear. It grabbed
me in the pit of my stomach and hung on. I wasn't afraid
of being alone in the house, but I became obsessed with
the fear that I might suddenly die and leave the children
orphans. I could see them—four waifs, sitting at the curb

begging. I recognize now that it was a normal reaction, but at the time I couldn't seem to share this feeling with anyone. I drove the car as little as possible, fearing a car accident. I was fearful of any activity that might lead to an accident. I feared illness. Every small symptom of ill health, whether constipation or loss of appetite or a twinge of gas, I interpreted as serious illness. I went to a lawyer to make a will and to have guardians appointed for my children. I lay awake at nights wondering how the children would fare if I died suddenly, and they were separated and placed into different homes. Would a new mother remember James' sensitivity to gruffness and Christine's need for extra love at bedtime?

Tangled with the dread of leaving the children complete orphans was the bewilderment at being single once again, of moving into society by myself. During the years of our marriage I had often looked with pitying eyes upon the single women and widows in the community. Although most married couples won't admit it openly, being married does make them feel superior to single persons.

In our sex-dominated society the acceptable standard in social life is a couple, though not necessarily a married couple. Single women will admit that society doesn't fully accept or make room for the single person, whether that single status is voluntary or not. Such people eventually learn that they must live on the periphery of society, out of the mainstream. "Substitute living," is what one single woman termed it. "I feel like a little girl with her nose pressed flat against the window of a candy shop," said another. "The church is geared to couples' classes, and mothers' classes, husbands' night, and family night. Where do I fit in? Nowhere!"

Like most widows, I found the fact that I was now an incomplete social unit one of the first difficult adjustments. I rebelled against this unconscious ostracism. Many hearts are big enough to accept a widow with her children into family gatherings, but few will help widows or single persons find their place as individuals in church and community. When I was invited to the homes of women my own age, it was usually when their husbands were away for business trips or other reasons.

One widow, who was part of a distinct social group by reason of her husband's profession and who because of his death was thrust out, spoke of frustrating "withdrawal pains." I had always been keenly interested in the church and its activities because of Walter's involvement and also my own concerns. Now, suddenly, I found that all contact with the church's decision-making processes had been cut off. I didn't like my own feelings when I gradually realized how much of the church is a male domain, especially its boards, committees, and so forth. Those were the feelings of a feminist and I felt repelled by them, yet sitting outside the gate felt just as awkward. From the first I struggled not to be sucked into the cluster of widows within the church who sat silently in their pews each Sunday, spectators to the work of God, contributing what they could from time to time as opportunity opened to them. They didn't appeal to me at all, but I was now one of them.

Loneliness is one of life's most crushing emotions. The battle of most widows against loneliness is constant. It takes working at, for every normal woman has a heart hunger to share her life with someone she loves and needs, and who loves and needs her. Now, that person is gone.

"We're sure lonely now, aren't we?" asked my little son quietly one hot summer evening the first summer after Walter had died, as he and I sat down to supper. His three sisters had left that afternoon for a lengthy vacation in Canada at the homes of my sisters and their families. They had offered to care for the girls for the summer months. James had remained with me.

Tears stung my eyes. Lonely? Even a little fellow could sense that one mother and one little boy don't make a family. Yet to keep that "family feeling" is all important, or the family broken by death may suffer complete breakdown.

What most widows miss isn't the security of life with a husband, nor the exciting moments such as a trip to Florida, nor new purchases made together like a new car. I found I missed most the privilege of sharing life with someone—at the end of a weary day to know again the gentle touch of a dear hand and to tell someone what the day had been. I wanted a person there to touch and to hold and to be with.

One family had for years been burdened by a nagging debt which in spite of careful budgeting couldn't be paid. When the father in the home suddenly died, his life insurance covered this debt. The day his wife came into the house with the canceled note in her hand, the urge to tell him overcame her. "Henry," she shouted, "I've paid it. We don't owe that money any more." The words fell empty at her feet. Henry was gone. Often during the day I heard a bit of news about a former friend and hastily reminded myself to tell Walter about it that evening. Then I had to remind myself afresh that no one was waiting at home to hear that David and Jennie were buying a new business or that Dan had finally received the Ph.D. degree he'd been working on for so many years. Walter was dead.

Watching the closeness of other couples gave me excruciating pain at first. One evening several friends invited me to attend the local fireworks display with them on July 4. The evening went well with much good conversation and laughter. Then, as darkness fell and the fireworks decorated the heavens, a strange sentimental atmosphere settled on the group and couples pulled together. I stood off by myself and watched a friend slip his arm around his wife. They snuggled together as they watched a Roman candle illuminate the sky. The pain was almost too much.

Loneliness is both a sudden thing and a creeping thing. Days went by and I thought I'd conquered the problem. Then suddenly I saw a piece of my husband's writing, or someone who looked like him passed by, and loneliness descended like a flood. During the first months I found I wept at anything: a familiar song, a faint memory, a picture of old times. I avoided playing the piano which I used to do by the hour while Walter studied and the children got ready for bed. Funerals were devastating to me, especially of young fathers. Yet at other times I could visit a young widow and feel no emotion, as though the gift of tears had been lost entirely. I knew her feelings—the crushing sorrow at the loss of your chosen companion for life, the sense of being suddenly picked up and flung against a stone wall to fall bleeding and broken to the earth. But I couldn't communicate my feeling, nor could I understand the strange mixture of emotions within me.

Just when you think you have conquered a certain problem, another crops up. You expect to be lonely. But you aren't prepared to fight the attitude of bitterness that insidiously moves into your life. In the years since my husband's death, I've seen the root of bitterness develop into monstrous ugly tubers in the spirit of some widows. They lash out against life, against friends, even against God, crying, "Why? Why?" I had faced the problem of bitterness and self-pity the year Walter studied at Syracuse. I knew now that unless I conquered this enemy early in my widowhood, life would become unbearable for me and the children.

Suffering draws us closer to God or it embitters. A person can't remain the same. Psychologists say that an individual can't hold two strong emotions at the same time. A person can't be bitter about life and full of joy simultaneously. Some widows feel they have the right to be bitter. Death has robbed them of their claim to a complete family life, to happiness, financial security, and so forth. But bitterness doesn't come from death or loss; it is born in our hearts. It's never worth the cost to our own lives and those of friends and family. The energy consumed in being bitter toward life over "what might have been" is better used to improve life now.

Feelings of loneliness, bitterness, and insecurity in a social situation may also cause a widow to withdraw from society and to build walls to keep from getting hurt again. Sorrow, which should make us more open to others and to God, becomes a selfish thing like the Dead Sea, giving up nothing and becoming so saturated with hard feelings that people find no reason to come close to the person going through it.

At times I felt I had answers to the problems of bitterness and self-pity and was satisfied in my spirit that by the grace of God I had overcome. Then doubts and questionings would come back, and the battle had to be fought each day, the answers found once again and rehearsed to myself, and my inner spirit revived. Theological questions about death and healing and suffering would have to be answered later. For the time being I pushed them aside until I had more time for thinking.

I didn't want to be bitter, yet time and again I wondered why such a snuffing out of a life obviously yielded to Christ was necessary. How could the death of a young father glorify the work of God? The change in our vocational plans was just as difficult to accept. For almost fifteen years Walter and I had pursued the goal of religious journalism. Now it had once again become a will-o'-the-wisp on the horizon. Though I had personally considered moving into the field, I soon found that the conservative denomination to which I belonged didn't have the same open doors for a woman that it had for men. Though religious journalism had been my husband's goal in life, I would have to find other ways of supporting my family and serving God. Suddenly life which had had clear goals and purposes became a wasteland. I didn't know what to do or how to do what I should be doing.

Among the emotions a widow has to contend with is guilt. I was plagued with guilt about a number of matters. Had I seen to it that Walter had received the best medical attention? When he first became ill, why hadn't I pushed the matter of a complete physical examination? Should I have called for more professional advice even though our family doctor had advised against spending more money for medical help later in the illness?

Then once in awhile I was reminded of arguments and quarrels we'd had over the years. There was the time he had slept on the couch and I hadn't slept at all. The time we couldn't agree on a pair of shoes. If I could manage to forget about the disagreements and regard them as normal, I was tempted to turn Walter into a paragon without any human faults. He was kind, gentle, loving, considerate, brilliant. Yes, he was, but then I would feel guilty when the maleness of men I met suddenly overwhelmed me. Where was my loyalty to the man I'd slept with only a few months ago?

At this moment my only real regret is that Walter and I didn't spend more time together. For many years we were both so caught up in church activities and family problems that our time for one another was shoved aside until later. And then it was too late.

Although I can smile now at some of the other incidents of that first year, I recognize how a person in mourning can be affected by community expectations. A person in grief, for example, is expected to wear a certain type of clothing to the funeral and immediately thereafter. I knew too little about death, and the customs related to death and dying, to recognize that even our small, strongly church-oriented community had expectations that I might not be fulfilling and of which I wasn't aware until much later. I know now that I was expected to place a formal thank-you note in the local paper addressed to doctors, nurses, hospital staff, and all who sent cards, foods, and so forth. I neglected to do so. I sent them personally.

Each Memorial Day, the citizens of the community honor the memory of the dead by placing masses of plastic flowers (and a few fresh ones, if the season is early) on the graves of loved ones. The cemeteries become a riot of color. I refused to do so because ugly plastic wreaths didn't fit my memory of Walter as a man who shortly before had been alive and full of vibrant ideas. One year I found that someone else had put them there for me. Perhaps Walter's grave looked too lonely.

I have never felt much compulsion to visit Walter's grave. Walter is not there; only his remains are. I hold little emotional attachment to that spot in the Gnadenau cemetery two miles south of town, so I go there seldom. I remember a young friend from years ago whose fiancé had died shortly before their wedding. She had dozens of pictures taken of herself weeping at the grave. She had surrounded herself in her grief with these pictures and prolonged the separation.

I have also heard of other widows who for years left their husband's personal possessions and room the way it had been at his death. They refused to disturb this shrine to his memory. Yet each passing month can make it more difficult to get rid of memories with the mementos. Before Walter's brothers and sisters left for their distant homes, I had already decided that his clothing, which had never meant much to him, could be theirs if they wanted it. The afternoon before their departure I spread his clothes out on the bed and suggested they help themselves: shirts, suits, the new black size 12 shoes that didn't fit anyone, socks, underwear, sweaters. I reserved a few personal items to give to the children later on and donated the leftovers to a church relief society.

His personal effects were more difficult to deal with. I sold some of his books I knew I would never use. His letters, journals, sermon outlines, course outlines, and so forth took several years to work through and were more painful to deal with because they represented the person-hood of my husband as his clothing never had.

The community expects grief of the widow, but it also expects victory. If there are no tears, something is wrong. The wise widow knows how to show this proper balance. But who is wise at such a time? I cringed the first weeks under the question, "How are you getting along?" which suggested that as a widow I should be having difficulty. I was, but I wasn't ready to share my personal feelings with every questioner. In later years I was able to counter with, "How are *you* getting along?" chuckling inwardly while the questioner stumbled for an answer, perhaps wondering if I had some inside knowledge about the state of her emotional well-being.

A sense of humor helps very much. In time the children and I developed our own widow jokes, but not at the beginning. Then it was too painful, like digging into a festering boil. New widows should be warned against busybodies who outwardly visit in the name of Christ but who actually come in the interests of their own curiosity, prying for juicy information about the widow's emotional state to pass on at the next stop as a prayer request. Eventually I learned whom I could trust with personal information and which people I had to treat with extra patience and grace. Some offered glib comfort with words such as "The Lord knew who could take such an experience", others listened quietly. The most comforting words I can remember came from a tiny, elderly widow with a twinkle in her eye. She laid a hand gently on mine and said, "It will not always be like this." I found that some people actually enjoyed having in their midst a poor widow with many children so they could feel useful. Others loved us for our own sake. That knowledge was another step in my recovery.

I don't remember the first time we laughed together about widowhood, but I do recall one Christmas when we received an unexpected gift basket of fruit and candy, gaily wrapped in colored cellophane, from the deacons of the church. The children and I thoroughly enjoyed the surprise. But when the same gift arrived year after year at Christmas, we came to expect what we referred to in the family as our "widow basket." The bigger joke happened several years later when Roger, my son-in-law, who was courting my daughter Susan at the time, arrived on Christmas Eve carrying a replica of the widow basket which was already sitting on the dining room table.

Many widows wrote to me during the first year and also later on. They told me that God had never forsaken them. One young widow whose husband had died shortly after her twin babies were born said that God had never failed to supply all needs, spiritually, physically, and financially.

At the end of that year I had a little clearer understanding of the fact that death is universal. I hadn't been picked out for some special punishment from God. Sickness and death are part of the human lot. Life never moves ahead without a ripple. There had been problems before; there would be problems now. It's easy to talk about "resting in the Lord" but I learned that resting in

God doesn't depend on outward circumstances, but on one's relationship to Christ.

I had some good memories of my life together with Walter. I appreciated the many letters I received from his friends relating some of their remembrances of him. A nun, a fellow classmate at Syracuse University, wrote: "You have much to be proud of in your husband; your children have a fine example to live up to. I often sympathized with Walter last year that he had to be away from the family he so loved. I never dreamed that he had a far more difficult cross to bear, in his illness. His courage and cheerfulness and hope in the face of it are a source of inspiration to me now, as they must be to others, for never once did he let us suspect that he was not well. It may ease your sorrow somewhat to learn that those of us who knew him here saw only a strong, rather quiet man who went steadily about his business from day to day, kind and affable, keeping his burden to himself. Now more than ever it seems to me that he was a man to his fingertips, a Christian gentleman with great faith in his Maker, and hope in his heart that the God who made the illness could also make all things right, in his own way and time."

I bore the burden of wondering what he might have been able to achieve had God permitted him to live. I shared the perplexity of widows such as Mrs. Jacqueline Kennedy, Mrs. Coretta King, and others whose husbands were statesmen, writers, artists, or leaders in their field. What might Walter have accomplished had he lived? These are questions without answers.

I remember clearly the first anniversary of my husband's death (if one can speak of it as an anniversary), and the tremendous feeling of exultation I had that we had crossed the first mountain, difficult as it had been. God had been gracious; we were thankful. I realized that friends expected grief of me on this day of remembrance. It was there, but it was intermingled with praise for the beginning lessons I had learned. We hadn't flunked the course. I could affirm Oswald Chamber's words: "If your cup is pleasant, be thankful. If your cup is bitter, drink it in communion with God." I didn't know what the years ahead would bring, but for the present I could only commit them to God.

Like most young couples, Walter and I had planned for years of life together. Like most couples, we had almost entirely left out one factor in our consideration. It is this: Barring a motor accident or other disaster in which both husband and wife are killed instantaneously, the day will come when one partner will be left alone. In most cases it will be the wife. Not only do women have a longer life expectancy than men, but because they frequently marry men older than themselves, the husband usually dies first. So, as one writer put it, the bride who hasn't made a study of widowhood is in many ways less prepared for life than the one who doesn't know how to diaper a baby.

Social security, insurance, job opportunities take care of most of the financial needs of the woman left alone. But there are deep needs of the spirit also. A widow gropes with the question of the ultimate destiny of her husband's soul, with pressing problems of life without his physical presence in a society that denies a full life to a person without a partner.

I realized that part of the answer to a widow's affliction lies in herself and God. "Now she that is a widow indeed, and desolate, trusts in God" (1 Timothy 5:4). To accept her new role in life without bitterness requires divine grace. Spiritual vision is myopic when life is lived in the dull gray shades of sorrow and grief. Only the knowledge that the sovereign God cradles the world in the palm of his hand brings life into proper perspective and opens new avenues of service when the spirit protests, "Life isn't fair." Dividends will come when one who has met the sting of death with the truth, "I am the resurrection, and the life," is enabled to turn affliction into victory.

But these answers weren't fully mine yet.

Part
Two

CHAPTER FOUR
Who Am I?

Simon Peter said unto him, Lord, whither goest thou?
(Quo vadis, Domine?) —John 13:36

Before Walter died I had begun formulating for myself certain tenets of my own faith and life philosophy, writing them down, revising them as new light came to me.

I had discovered that I was responsible for my own sin and Christian commitment. I couldn't hide behind the merits of a father, a husband, or children, much as I would like to at times. Life may be simplest when lived within the safe confines of a house, with no contact with the outside world except quick safe trips to church. Yet if I never gave of myself to others, although there would be fewer conflicts in life I could also expect few rewards.

I had learned that I was responsible to God for my life, all of it. To deny part of it, particularly my intellect, as our culture pressures women to do, and to become a mere feminine appendage to male endeavors, decorating the environment and pleasant to have around, was to deny myself the way God had made me, and therefore in some sense was to deny God himself. However, I couldn't deny responsibility to husband and children either, for I had chosen marriage and family.

I had discovered that full identity is possible in Christ Jesus and that the teachings of the Bible grant me the right to unique personhood. My long and difficult pilgrimage did not end with widowhood. I learned that I needed a central core of strength not provided by the culture (with its emphasis on sex and vacuity for women), nor by the church (with its emphasis on woman's limitations), nor by the demands of being a woman (wife, mother, and widow later on). That strength came only as I regarded myself the way God sees me: a person whose faith is in the atoning work of Christ on the Cross.

I had to think of myself as a believer in persons, at least for a time, until my thinking balanced out. Even now, when the subject of women's liberation comes up, I find that people occasionally drop me into that category, albeit with an apologetic laugh. I wince a little, for I have never considered myself a feminist. I realize that it is incredibly difficult to help people sort out their attitudes on this touchy subject. Some people would call me a feminist, because I openly advocate that men and women join the human race. I am a believer in persons. If I'm a feminist, I must testify that Christianity has influenced my feminism. I am what I am because I have accepted Christ's words of liberation for all humankind.

I have refused to read the Bible with a sexist sieve, subconsciously relegating one passage to men and the next to women. As I accepted God's Word as a message to myself, a person, I discovered that God looks at each of us as an individual, not as male or female, Jew or Greek,

white or black. People are concerned with these limitations, not God.

As I was beginning to sort out these ideas, I wasn't
prepared for the battering of spirit I went through when
Walter died. I thought I had most of my concepts well
filed and tabulated for ready reference in my mind. Yet I
am reassured now that the inner life ends when the quest
for identity is abandoned and the individual is satisfied to
coast along. Each new stage in a person's experience must
be accepted for what it can contribute to inner growth.
And at first I could not see how widowhood could
contribute much besides ugliness. Most people think that
identity crises are only for adolescents moving into adulthood. It took several years as a widow for me to realize
that what I had struggled through was an identity crisis
not unlike that of a teen-ager. Other widows have told
me of going through the same terrifying and humiliating
experience of suddenly being bereft of an identity, like
being made to stand naked in the city square. Many of
them were almost reluctant to talk about it, as if it were
something shameful. Widows who before their husband's
death were engaged in an occupation that gave them an
identity in their own right, and who have enjoyed relationships separate from their husbands, may not have
quite the same difficulty. But those of us who have found
satisfaction in remaining in the background of our
husband's life feel like a drowning child.

The day Walter died, I knew I was a widow, yet I had
no image in my mind of myself as a widow. I had no
satisfactory role models before me. What was a widow
like? What was expected of her in behavior and service?
My sister provided me with a black dress and hat and

gloves, but beyond these outward symbols, what was widowhood? Shadowy images of silent, lonely women, hovering in the background of society and life, drifted through my thoughts. Was that what I actually was now? I didn't know much about widows, but I knew that I had to be terribly strong for a while, at least until the children were older. I had leaned a lot on Walter for many years, even while struggling for answers to personal questions. I knew I had to "get my head together" as young people say today, but I didn't know how.

Identity is usually thought of as knowing who you are, where you're going, and what you're doing with your life. Traditionally people find their identity in some vocational goal or in their relationship to other persons. Ask someone who he or she is. The response is usually "I'm a teacher," or "I'm a housewife," or "I'm a wife and mother." Many women will respond with the latter two answers, but few men will first answer "I'm a father," or "I'm a husband." Their response is usually their vocation.

Previously, if someone had asked me who I was, I would have answered quite naturally, "I'm Mrs. Walter Wiebe" or "I'm a wife and mother." Those answers were satisfactory to me. I *was* a wife and mother. I was trying to combine those roles with writing, but I felt too timid to speak of myself as a writer.

After Walter's death, some persons insisted on calling me Mrs. Walter Wiebe, because Amy Vanderbilt said that's the way a widow should be referred to. Yet I knew, and they knew, that I was no longer Mrs. Walter Wiebe. Walter was dead. How could I be the wife of a dead man?

Suddenly I had lost my role. I retained the name, but it was an empty title. I had no concept of my true identity. I was a nothing. A total blah. I couldn't answer the question, Who are you? I never answered Mrs. Walter Wiebe as I heard other widows do, for that answer shrieked a lie. He was dead, dead, dead. Though I still had the children, I had lost the wife role, and society doesn't recognize the mother role as it does that of the wife. If the children are grown and important, this may be a satisfactory substitute, but not otherwise. John F. Kennedy's mother, Mrs. Rose Kennedy, has a public identity largely because of her son. I was the mother of four young children.

The future closes in sharply when one has no identity, like the final curtain at the end of a bad stage play. A widow lacks a feeling of self-worth unless she can identify herself to other people in some way. She has to be able to say something in response to the question, "Who are you?" and yet "I am a widow" is no answer. What is a widow?

Older persons approaching retirement face a similar problem. One day they are gainfully employed. On the day of retirement after receiving a gold watch or corsage, a certificate of long-term employment, and maybe a pension, they lose the role that gave life meaning. They have to admit to themselves, I am retired. I am no longer a contributing member of society. And unless they find some meaningful activity to give them a new identity they suffer endlessly. Being a retiree as yet doesn't seem to have enough prestige to count as an identity.

Others facing this strange nameless problem are individuals suddenly unemployed. Who is a carpenter if he has no job? "Unemployed" lacks the ring of worth. Wives can lose their sense of self-worth if pushed too far into submissive roles and denied a voice in the family's decision-making process. Some young people experience loss of identity through repeated failure at some course in school, in a vocation, or in a family relationship.

If being a widow gave the woman prestige and worth in the eyes of society, perhaps women would say it more proudly. But too often to be a widow means you are nothing.

A new widow will find herself clinging to the old identity as the wife of her husband with the tenacity of contact cement. She doesn't want to be single, for she enjoyed the old way of living. She developed an identity in her marriage that determined who she was, what she did, when she did it, and with whom she established her social relationships. Marriage was a way of living for two people who had committed themselves to becoming a unit. It supplied reasons for living and rules for the way life was lived.

The widow must develop a new image of herself as a single person, even while she tends to think of herself as a married person. She may cling to the old image and hope that her friends and acquaintances do likewise. She may not realize that their view of her has changed. When they overlook her basic social need to be one of the old group of mixed friends, she may get the message that no longer being a wife means no longer being a person.

This awareness came to me in little ways, yet each small clue had the force of a chisel blow, stripping me of my old identity without helping me find a new one. Friends of my husband who would have stopped at our home for a meal and a visit now found it inconvenient to do so. Those who saw my husband as the most worthwhile person in our friendship now passed me by completely, as if I didn't exist in their thinking anymore. I felt at times as if I'd been sent into Siberian exile. As my social patterns changed completely over a course of several years, I stood there like a child trying to wave down the train with a pocket handkerchief, wondering why I wasn't going along. Another widow in our community had the same bewildering experience. We shared notes and cried together.

Women who by virtue of their husband's work have been deeply involved in church and civic organizations are sometimes most confused by the sudden loss of identity. Dropping them from guest lists, committee meetings, and newsletters may not be consciously cruel. But to the unsuspecting widow it will feel as if someone has lopped off her hands and feet with a giant butcher knife and left her immobile.

One widow whose husband was a deacon with whom she had often visited the sick, elderly, and needy, found that the church no longer recognized her contribution to what had been a man-wife team. She was no longer part of the spiritual force of the deacons in the church.

Women whose husbands were ministers and pastors speak with nostalgia about the time when the parsonage was the center of activity: guests, missionaries, speakers, congregational members coming and going. A pastor dies and his wife is shoved to the sidelines to watch what is going on. One minister's wife told me how she and her husband had always been the first to church to greet people. Now no one cared when she arrived.

The wife of a missionary who struggled through the call to the mission field as much as her husband did may find that when he dies, her services are discontinued and she and her family are on a fast plane to America. Here she may work eight hours a day at a job to help support the family. Why couldn't she continue to give that energy to the work of God? There is no answer.

I didn't understand the void in my life following Walter's death until much later, when I could view more objectively what was taking place. I was being forced to make my reentry into a society that didn't care whether I was coming back or not.

I was being pushed into the business world which was foreign to me. I had been a housewife and mother, familiar with dishes and casseroles and a quiet life of reading and writing. My main activity for about fifteen years had been the care and feeding of children and husband. My skills as an office worker were rusty. I felt awkward when meeting new people, especially professional people—those smartly dressed women who knew how to keep their hair neat for a whole day and blouse fronts free from spots from hastily prepared meals. Taking the big step into the working world made me feel like a clown performing before a disinterested audience.

For four years I worked as an editorial assistant in a publishing house, doing copy editing and proofreading. My husband, who had been a member of the board of this publishing house, had usually discussed with me at great length the concerns of a small denomination's religious publishing. I was as much interested in seeing the cause of Christian literature grow as he was. When I became an employee, I found that I knew less about the administrative details than when I'd had no official connection. The incongruity was both amusing and dismaying. I had naively expected to become part of the creative force that would move the work ahead; my employer saw me only as a woman who needed some way to earn a living and not as a person with deep commitment to journalism.

I wish I'd known then, as I do now, that recovery from grief after the death of a close family member and "finding oneself" is both a crisis and a process, and that it has its own time schedule. Each widowed individual faces more or less the same problems, but some with greater intensity than others. Widowhood is a tragedy only when death becomes both the end of living for the husband and an end in itself for her. It's a humble victory when it begins a period of self-awareness and growth, when the widow finds grace to create a new life and to improve upon the past—harsh as this may sound. This doesn't mean turning one's back upon the past. Marriage was good. Now the agenda is different and one must make beauty out of the ashes. Many widows are forced to grow in their personalities because of the decisions they must now make alone. One person commented that all "successful widows" stuck in his craw, especially if they became a success in the area of work in which their husbands had been active. The truth is that many widows receive a new assignment from the Lord after their husbands' deaths. Even if it puts them into the spotlight, the motive is seldom to show up their husbands.

As a widow, I didn't fit in with single women, for they were free to come and go more or less as they pleased. I had four children who needed me. I didn't fit in with older widows without children. They had their own groups, activities, and interests, which didn't interest me. I wasn't married, yet I wasn't single. I wasn't entirely a housewife, yet I wasn't a career woman. I was working to make a living for myself and the children, but I knew I had to find something to give me satisfaction and satisfy my basic commitment to Christ and his work.

It took me several years to begin to feel at home with myself as a person and to recognize the direction God was leading me. I did much searching, yet I had heavy guilt feelings about changing our original plans to move into religious journalism.

Thinking of going back to school, I faced the kind of identity crisis that men face early in life. Our culture expects them to push into the future pursuing a career image that they admire. They choose a profession and move into it gradually but steadily with the full encouragement of family and friends. Women are not expected to move into a career so deliberately.

I had once chosen marriage and a family, and dabbled in writing. Now I had to choose a career just like a man, which frightened me. I couldn't go back only to homemaking. That decision was made for me by my financial situation. I had to face what to do with my life for the next twenty or more years, and I knew I didn't want to spend it behind a desk proofreading and copy editing. I had to find a self-image I could respect and live with for a long, long time. I feared not being myself, yet I was also afraid of being myself—whoever that was—but then not getting the respect and recognition I cherished from those I respected. What a tangle.

What did I want from the years ahead? Money? Power? Love? Fame? Security? What did God want of me? Could one ask that question of him even after one's teen-age years?

The basic identity of a Christian comes from knowing

and doing the will of God. I did a lot of reading about maturity, having much growing up to do in a hurry. The suddenness with which I was thrown into the working world demanded a quickie course.

I learned that a Christian must assume personal responsibility for mental and spiritual growth until death. He or she must develop an individual plan for life-long learning. Too many middle-aged people have stopped learning, have hung onto old concepts, and then have become defensive and frightened by changes. I had enough to be fearful about, so I had to learn to change and swing with the blows. The way of growth is not in standing still.

Books on church renewal published at that time were stressing "Say Yes to Life" for all believers. On the other hand, I had to consider the conditioning of childhood and church teachings which seemed to say that women didn't need to move ahead, at least not much. Men, yes. But women needed only to be submissive and passive. Independence and initiative were regarded as masculine qualities. I repeatedly faced the question of how a widow could survive without initiative, even on such mundane matters as car repair.

People who know me now don't usually think of me as a fearful person. They are unaware of how I inched my way through a multitude of fears. Sometimes I would struggle with myself for hours before making a phone call to do an interview for an article. When I began teaching, I felt so insecure that I wrote out every word of every lecture. I didn't feel confident enough to speak extemporaneously.

When I gave a public talk, even a very informal one, I

trembled for a long time afterward. When asked to speak before a mixed group, I never knew how to respond.

I read articles that heaped guilt on working mothers, assuring them that their children would not turn out well. I wondered what I could do to escape that punishment.

I despised articles that criticized women for performing any service that might take a man's work from him.

Any recital of such experiences tends to come out sounding negative. But it is bewildering to have had an identity, be robbed of it, and then be forced to look for it like the boy who lost his shadow.

The easiest way out of the situation would have been to avoid the responsibility of making decisions. I could have accepted everyone else's advice and simply drifted with circumstances.

In searching for my new identity I found considerable help from books for divorcees. Writers of these books were more willing to accept the gut-level realities of life than writers of religious books for widows. Getting back into society was an absolute necessity for me, as it is for all widows. Yet many widows, like myself, are unwilling to shout for help and therefore bob around in the deep water about to drown. I've wondered since if we Christians are humiliated to find ourselves so inadequate for the new role thrust upon us. We have the mistaken idea that God wants "perfect widows" who meet every problem with aplomb, grace, and fortitude, rather than persons who know their weakness, trust him for help, and aren't afraid to ask for it from him or his children.

Gradually, I found that I was achieving an identity not as a widow, but as a person. If people referred to me as a widow, I didn't mind. That was their problem. God didn't see me that way first of all, any more than he saw Anna the prophetess as a widow.

My new life brought me more and more out of the home and into the world into which I had previously sent my husband and children. I had to do more questioning about matters I had accepted as natural to the Christian life when I didn't have to test them personally. I found I had to learn to accept the children as individuals. Life became easier when they weren't the total focus of my life. Family living became more relaxed. Although I had found it easy to give my children pat answers about what to do when they collided headlong with moral and social issues (sexual freedom, abortion, the pill, marijuana, protest marches, famine, homosexuality, etc.), now I came into personal contact with some of these issues.

Together with my children I asked searching questions: Is God still alive? Is his arm really not shortened? Why then does he let us go through such difficult experiences? Where is the church? I found myself discarding as extra baggage much that had seemed important at one time: running to every meeting, being seen at certain functions, being a part of everything expected of a church family, putting security in things like furniture, a car, clothing.

Yet in discarding the excess baggage, I found myself returning again and again to the words of Peter which I had first read as a young person. Many were forsaking Christ for other interests. Christ asked Peter, "Will you also go away?" Peter answered, "To whom shall we go? You alone have the answer to eternal life."

Widowhood, like any kind of living, required a faith that would cost me my life. I had to let go of all former securities and strengths to find the new securities God had for me.

I thank the men and women who encouraged me to go on to school and later helped me learn the ropes of teaching in a small church-related college. To learn the politics of a church institution, whether a school or a board (though they are extolled as being apolitical), is a school in itself. Again I felt like a kindergartner learning to write. I learned that there are always kind and considerate men around—someone to tell you whom to see for help. I learned how to tell who actually runs the institution from the person who says he does. I learned which people pick up your cause, which consider you as an equal, and which are frightened and threatened. Though church politics are kept as saintly as possible, humanity shows through when faith gets thin. I found it best to laugh and enjoy the absurdities of life instead of weeping too much about its incongruities.

To have found a safe place of my own as a person, not merely as a woman or as a widow, makes me highly vulnerable to criticism, as any person on a similar pilgrimage soon finds. Yet I am upheld by the word that everyone must give account of himself or herself before God (Romans 14:12)—and that includes the married, single, widowed, or divorced. And it includes all of life, not just that which occurs before death moves into a family.

My sister asked me how I liked being middle-aged, even though she is only four years younger. I didn't take long to answer. "I like it," I said. "I like the view."

I like being able to stand on this high point in the middle of life and look back without fear on what has happened. I think of myself as a mountain climber who has stopped temporarily en route to the top. I see the valleys, rocks, crevasses, crumbly places. It's all there, but I've been over it. The way ahead will be equally rough, but I have the satisfaction of knowing I have made it this far. The view is glorious.

From this point I can look back, but the pathway still leads up. This place of security, I know now, will never be the same from year to year. When the children all leave home, I may face another identity crisis. I will be tempted to settle down in my office-bedroom and shut out the world. Retirement and old age will bring other new adjustments but I am resolved never to settle down permanently. The only true security is in Christ, not in circumstances.

CHAPTER FIVE
Pushed out of Noah's Ark

"There went in two and two unto Noah into the ark, the male and the female, as God had commanded Noah" (Genesis 7:9)

I asked a few friends to tell me what words came to mind when they thought of the word *widow*.

"Lonely."

"Useless."

"Empty."

A friend mentioned that his wife had suggested they visit some of the older widows of the church. "Ohhh, no!" was his immediate response. "Let's not use up a free evening like that." The job description of most pastors includes "visiting the widows." I can remember from the shoptalk of my pastor-husband and his friends years ago how they shrank from widow-visiting. They regarded it as time spent unfruitfully. The job had to be done, but they'd rather not.

Widows, particularly older ones, aren't considered a highly productive group in the church. They are people you do things for, not with. Widows are for visiting. They have no particular assignment in the church, though many are obviously healthy, wealthy, and wise. Their most serious problem is that they're without a husband, which somehow incapacitates them to be part of the "with" group. Some are forced into a role from which there is no escape. Once a widow, always a widow—unless marriage changes the situation.

The apostle James in his epistle drew attention to widows, not because they were unmarried, but because they were symbolic of the helpless and oppressed of humanity. In our couple-oriented society, one is married or single before one is a person. James was writing about persons who had been hurt by the oppression of that unjust society. In our present society, widows are oppressed even by the church. The widow is placed in a special class because she is unmarried—not necessarily because of her psychological, spiritual, or financial need.

Some new widows feel they have no alternative but to slump into the widows' pew and wait for the dubious benefits accompanying the role: the visits by pastors and deacons, and the sympathy from all. Widows are seldom reminded that after they have done their "grief work"—which is necessary—they must move beyond widowhood back into life. The lonely widow role is only temporary; the role of personhood continues through life. But the way out of widowhood is difficult except by the grace of God. The conventions of society, both inside and outside the church, are strong, pushing the widow into a role society feels comfortable with.

I've talked to both single women and widows about the status of widows in the church. Some were reluctant to speak, not wanting to sound whining or critical. Shouldn't a person whose satisfactions are in the Lord have no complaints? Yet it became clear that little and sometimes big things convinced the widow that she had been gently shunted aside in church life.

Item: An invitation to a supper meeting reads, "Bring your spouse," or if it's from a women's group: "Bring your husband." What does the husbandless woman do? She stays home even though later she is assured that the invitation didn't mean what it said. She could have come alone, but coming alone means being the odd one, the one for whom someone must find an extra chair at a table set for four. Square tables don't allow for an extra person and few churches have round ones.

Item: Banquet tickets are $4.50 each or $8.00 for two—but the two have to be man and wife.

Item: The minister mentions that a sudden financial need has come up. "Will all men please remain after church for a short session." Widows earning as much as, or more than, some men go home.

Requests for volunteers for service projects, not specifically in the domestic area, are often for couples. Many church committees or diaconates elect only husband-and-wife teams.

Widows listen to hundreds of sermons, class discussions, and the like, in which married couples' problems are aired, the assumption being made that all the adult listeners are married.

At meetings at which important decisions are made, the widow's voice is seldom heard, yet she has no husband of whom to inquire what is going on.

After years of such divisive treatment, many widows agree that it's hard to stay on board Noah's ark as the survivor of a pair. In the church, where a widow should feel the most support and love, she often ends up feeling like a loser. Marriage is considered the norm, an obligation in our society, and almost the ticket for entrance into God's community.

"What shall we do with the single women?" asked one Sunday school teacher. "Let's keep them busy," was the quick, unthinking response of a member. One single woman told me later, "I could have cried right then. If we're busy, it takes us off their hands." Single women must be kept busy and widows must be visited.

Dr. Cynthia Wedel in *Working Women and the Church* writes, "All too often in its history the church has been so absorbed in its own institutional life and activity that it has failed to take account of changes in society until it has lost touch with great groups of people." Among the invisible people looking for a closer bond with the church are the singles: unmarried, widowed, and divorced. About 16.5 million women over 25 in this country are unmarried. About 4.2 million have never married and another 12.3 million have ended up separated, widowed, or divorced. About 10 percent ordinarily remain single.

As the lifespan increases, American women are becoming widows later in life and also are spending more years as widows. In 1890 the average woman was widowed in her early fifties but also died early. By 1960 the average woman was widowed at almost 64. In 1960 she faced an average of 15 years as a widow, and by 1970 an average of more than 18 years.

What does this trend mean for the church? Can the church afford to continue thinking of this growing body of women as a problem? How can it be helped to see them as one of the untapped resources for the work of the Kingdom?

I find that the development of this potential has been hindered by myths which combine to make widows feel like yesterday's tossed salad left uncovered in the noonday sun.

Myth No. 1: Widows and other single women are a breed apart with unique characteristics and can therefore be treated as a group. They can be herded into one Sunday school class, be invited out for supper as a group, or be offered the opportunity of fellowship as a unit.

Yet the truth is that single women have as much or as little in common as any group of married people. Their jobs, earning power, living arrangements, personalities, and life goals vary with the individual.

True, their single state may force them into seeking each other's company. The widow ghettos of the churches are an unchallenged fact. Lynn Caine in *Widow* writes that after her husband died she discovered this large community of "women who are alone". Widow after widow drops into it and stays there because she has no other social contacts.

Myth No. 2: All single women, whether single, widowed, or divorced, are husband-hunting or are treading water at their jobs and friendships "until I get married."

Not so, say the single women. Husband-hunting is not a priority for all. Some women have fully accepted and enjoy their single status; others have chosen it for the freedom it grants them for Christian service or vocational advancement.

Myth No. 3: All widows are poor, and all single women are rich. A columnist in a religious periodical, analyzing the stewardship of the churches, broke down each membership roll into three categories: those below age 65, those over age 65, and the widows. Obviously these latter were too poor to give.

In the Old Testament, widows were poor because of inheritance laws that passed their husband's estate to others. In the New Testament, they fared little better. On through the ages and particularly in the eighteenth and nineteenth centuries when husbands died early deaths, penury and widowhood kept close company. Even today many widows are desperately poor, including some in the church. The poorest of the poor is the black, single, old woman. She has four strikes against her. But many widows are adequately provided for by pension plans, social security, insurance, inheritances, and employment.

As I talked to widows of all ages, I sensed deep-seated yearnings some found difficult to articulate, the hurt was so severe.

"We would like to be accepted as human beings," said one. "We are no different from anyone else."

Widows need the input of masculine thinking for balanced living. For this they need the help of marrieds, yet some couples hesitate to visit or invite a widow because "the man will have no one to talk to". Some men drop their wives off and then go to a ball game or read the newspaper while the women talk. Widows tell me of being invited only when husbands are gone or another family is present. The communication soon becomes clear that a widow is not a highly valued guest by herself.

Friends sometimes wonder why I hesitate to attend church suppers and banquets. I don't enjoy going by myself. It's as simple as that. It becomes uncomfortable to be sifted out of the crowd to sit at the table with the people who don't fit into the coupled society.

At one large supper gathering I found myself and my children and another manless woman ushered to the children's table. I dismissed the matter as inconsequential. When, on another occasion, the incident nearly repeated itself and when another widow told me that the same thing had happened to her, I began to understand that to some people a widow doesn't really count as an adult. I almost understood then what a black person must feel when facing the sign "White Only."

At another large banquet a woman friend and I agreed to go together. As we entered the banquet hall, the ushers asked us if we would mind splitting up and taking single seats left here and there among couples. I wondered later how many married couples had been asked to do the same.

A widow may find herself in a peculiar situation with some men. They may treat her with a kind of reverse *Playboy* philosophy. *Playboy* readers are led to think of women as sexual objects, to be desired and used, but not to be regarded as persons. Some men cannot think of women, especially widows, except as sexual objects to be avoided. Every widow is a Merry Widow to them, a potential force for evil, rather than a person with integrity. Such men are like the preacher of an earlier age who was going home in a heavy downpour in his old buggy, when he passed one of his lady parishioners. He stopped only long enough to give her his regrets that his wife wasn't with him before he whipped his horse along.

The problem can't be easily dismissed. A widow should

know that many wives are jealous of her single state and fear she may capture a husband's attention. In the years since Walter's death I have been reluctant to ask other women's husbands for help, for fear I might be misunderstood. Perhaps I have been too cautious. On the other hand I have appreciated men who considered me a person worth talking to, one who still had something to offer life even though I happened to be female.

What widows and other single women need, if the church is to utilize their potential, is less sympathy and more actual acceptance into the social life of the church. I sense the tremendous potential locked up in some widows, which has no outlet and which the church has not discovered. A few are women who have been through a shattering experience, but who remain forever numbed by the failure of fellow Christians to accept them as full members of the community of saints. These yearnings to be a close member of the family of God are strong. "People don't sense our need of fellowship," one widow said wistfully.

Certain areas of church work are out of bounds without a husband. Women find they cannot speak out in church without being considered aggressive, competitive, a "women's libber," or even shrewish. Yet without a husband to ask at home, "No news reaches me," said one widow, mourning her former close involvement in church activities.

Emphasis on family-centered programs creates problems for the church member who isn't in a complete family. Single adults, widows, children whose parents avoid church, divorced or separated church members, feel left out in such situations.

After nearly thirteen years, I think I've faced and conquered many of the problems, yet recently I noticed that I was reluctant to attend a weekend family retreat. In the end I stayed home because I was "too busy". Yet if I'd been honest with myself I'd have admitted I couldn't face an entire weekend of couple-activity, hoping that some unit would find enough room for me. Being a fifth wheel for a whole weekend had little drawing power.

How can the church find ways to break down barriers and meet needs of all members regardless of family status? How can the church learn to function as a substitute family, providing love and fellowship for those who have no family? How can all singles be brought from the spectators' benches to the playing floor? Certainly not by isolating widows and single people into separate classes and fellowship groups, or inviting them only by groups into homes as we frequently do foreign students. I'm sure most people in these social categories would much rather be considered a person than a foreign student, a single person, or a widow to whom one dispenses fellowship at an annual dinner.

I suggest that couples invite fringe individuals to church and other social functions, picking them up and returning them to their homes, so that they know they won't be stranded at any time, a fear of most single persons. "Where is there a couple who won't mind my sitting with them?" is a universal question with singles.

As I talk to widows, I sense a need for more church organizations to help them draw on their own resources to become contributing members of church and society. Some struggle too long to get back into the functioning world. Some never make it. Protestant churches would do well to organize a counterpart of Nain, a Roman Catholic organization that helps widowed persons meet their problems and build new lives. Widowhood is not expected to be a permanent role.

A number of secular organizations have been formed to help this group of women, which is increasing each year, cope with daily problems. One of the better known is Parents Without Partners. The Widow-to-Widow Program of the Widows Consultation Center in New York City helps the widow through the grief process and gives direction for the transition to a new role in life. "Visiting the widows in their affliction" takes on new meaning when it becomes more than temporary sympathy but provides the tools to join society as a contributing member.

I believe that much of the awkwardness of single living is compounded by the labels the church uses to separate people. As one person said, "Being single isn't so bad; it's the word that sounds so cruel." Can the church begin to question the validity of tagging Sunday school classes with "young marrieds" or "couples' classes," or of holding "sweetheart banquets" or "husband's night" if it expects widows to attend? In decades past, a woman might be called "Widow Brown" for the rest of her life, informing everyone of her marital state. Some people cling to terms like "old maid," "old girl," "widow woman," "colored," and "nigger." These words, all belonging to the same class of obscenities, keep people trapped in a limiting role Christ never intended any of his children to have.

Many widows are looking for more service opportunities, particularly Bible-study oriented fellowship groups, but they find it difficult to get into a mixed group. They are tired of being shunted into the choir or women's clubs. Most women's activities are geared to the interests and skills of women whose vocation is home-making. Many widows, particularly those below retire-ment age, spend most of their time in other areas out of necessity. Some think they should no more be expected to quilt and wrap bandages than an active businessman is expected to paint toys each week.

Above all, widows need encouragement to develop Christ-honoring life styles, for the urge to live selfishly comes easily when one is alone. The example of Lydia, the seller of purple, a woman who was involved in busi-ness and also in the church, needs to be upheld as a role model. The church has room for widows and their gifts.

Economist Sylvia Porter writes: "The trend toward more woman-headed households will continue to reach new peaks, for our whole population is living longer and women still are outliving men. It's more than time for us to wake up to this phenomenon in our society, to give it the searching analysis it demands, to find out what it means to all of us."

Any general trend in society is reflected in church life as well. For the church this trend means a large reservoir of individuals whose gifts can be developed to serve Christ. For the widow, one of the greatest challenges of her life will be to let God work in her life.

CHAPTER SIX
Pushed into the Boxing Ring

Ships are safe in harbor, but that is not what ships are built for—to rest calmly in a harbor. They only get barnacle-crusted that way. They are made to launch out into the deep.—Anonymous

I live in a small community of about 2,800 residents. The telephone directory lists about one hundred households headed by a "Mrs." Most of these are widows. Actually the number of widows is larger because a few list their phone numbers under their deceased husband's name and others live with relatives or in a home for the aged.

This isn't an unusual proportion of widows in a community with many churches, a retirement center, and a college. Some churches may count as many as 5 to 8 percent of their membership widows. As an experiment, I checked our church roll. Out of approximately 90 resident households, I found about 22 headed by a widow or single woman. The prevalence of widows in the church is one of the better-known statistics, but like the weather, not much can be done about it. The apostle Paul did try to regulate their relationship to the church by establishing the deacons. Not all churches follow his example.

Harsh as it may sound, widowhood is the inevitable destiny of most married women. A woman now can normally expect to outlive her husband by six to seven years. And because she is usually two or three years younger than he, she can expect to spend about nine years as a widow. Some will spend more; some less.

The United States has about ten million widows who have to worry about the plumbing when it plugs up as well as how to finance the college education of their children. Some have to worry about their own education. What each woman faces is different. No one really knows what widowhood will mean until it happens to her. Though many women recognize the possibility of widowhood, most are totally unprepared for it. Even women of seventy and eighty are as unready as a woman of thirty-five, and widowhood comes to these older women at an age when it's harder to cope because their physical and mental powers aren't as keen as before.

During the years since Walter died, I have seen my own widowhood and that of many other women of all ages from a variety of perspectives. In a sense I have become a widow-watcher. Although actual preparation for of widowhood at any moment is a morbid occupation to be avoided, a little understanding of what may lie ahead will make the rough road a little smoother. It can make the difference between bogging down in a rut of obsessive self-pity and finding that life lived with Christ holds new challenges if a person reaches out for them.

For some women, becoming a widow is like being pushed into a boxing ring. One look at their opponent makes them say, "Punch me once and I'll lie down for the count." A person in grief is tempted to surrender to adversity or make a truce with it. Self-pity is destructive. It can reach out to other members of the family as well, as the widow hugs them to herself to avoid open confrontation with society.

Widows have seldom received special counseling. Rebellious or maladjusted teen-agers, young married couples who can't get along with one another, even the newly-divorced are recognized as individuals who need special advice—as are alcoholics and drug addicts. But widows?

"The problem in American society—the extent that woman's identity is based on being a wife—is that the widow has no place to go," says Dr. Helena Zananiecki Lopata, an expert on widowhood. "She can't be a widow, really, and she can't go back to being single. If she can't be a wife, can't be a widow, can't be single, her identity has to come from something else."

The fewer resources a woman had as a wife, the less she is able to cope as a widow. Dr. Lopata's advice for those wanting to help widows is "to help them to help themselves." Help them become independent, she says.

To a woman who has been dependent on her husband for financial and emotional support as well as for moral and spiritual leadership, the goal of becoming independent sounds almost like disloyalty or infidelity. Some women who spent their total energy in homemaking while the children were young and their husbands alive, may now find their interests drawing them into areas such as music, art, painting, teaching or writing. They may suffer from a deep-seated feeling that moving on beyond the original family blueprint is antiscriptural.

Some kind friends intimated to me early in my widow-hood that I shouldn't expect too much more out of life. I had had one of life's good experiences, a satisfactory marriage. I "at least had the children." Why not settle for this? They seemed to suggest that I wait in the shadows instead of making new plans, getting an education, and reaching out for vocational goals as I was about to do. They were advising me to remain in the past. I rejected their advice.

Death robs a family of its hopes and dreams for tomorrow and leaves in their place only memories. To live only with memories is to enter a prison of our own making and shut the door to the future.

Viktor Frankl in *Man's Search for Meaning* shows this clearly. During the last world war, prisoners in German concentration camps who closed their eyes to the future and lived only in the past found no meaning in their pitiful existence and soon died. The prisoner who lost faith in the present and hope for the future was doomed. The one who saw that life expected something of him even in that grim situation could make an inner victory out of his experiences. "It did not matter what we expected of life," writes Frankl, himself a prisoner, "but rather what life expected from us."

Widowhood is like that. It doesn't matter what the widow expected of life—love and happiness, friends, travel, service opportunities. At the point of her husband's death, it matters only what life expects of her. If she's a Christian, it matters what God expects of her. And as Frankl says, when individuals find it in their destiny to suffer, they will have to accept suffering as their task. For a widowed person, this may be her task for awhile. But only for awhile. The death of her husband may always be a "toothache in her heart," but life expects more of her.

Even a woman whose husband's health is A-1 would be well advised to get some idea of the problems she might face should she be left alone. What property and stocks does he own? How much does he owe? To whom? How much insurance does he carry? Where does he keep his will and other documents? Where does he do his banking? How much has he been giving to the church and other charitable institutions? Who will guide her through the estate settlement? What friends can she count on keeping without a husband? These are not trivial matters when every decision must be made alone.

I suggest that every wife learn to ask questions and get answers about finances and real estate—and about cars and appliances. Find out which service people one might need to call. Learning some simple mechanical skills of living, like the difference between a two-ply and a four-ply tire, doesn't mean overthrowing a husband's headship, as some women think. It only helps them to learn to provide for themselves, to be more self-sufficient should their husband become sick or die. One older widow who lives in a modern house built for her by her children doesn't use the garbage disposal. She is afraid of it. Some like her carry on by sheer willpower and fear through a maze of legal documents and mechanical problems. How much easier life alone would be for them if earlier in life they had learned to live decisively with these complicated matters.

One of the first rounds in the boxing ring after death is

making funeral arrangements, a matter most couples would rather not discuss. Yet some frank discussion beforehand will make it easier, for not every funeral director treats the death like that of his own wife. One widow told me that after the accidental death of her husband in a distant state, she actually had to hassle with a funeral director to keep from being forced to accept his decisions. He was aware that she was weak from the accident herself.

The inevitable question after a death is "What happens now?" Closely connected to it is the question of money. A young father suffered a heart attack. His brother's wife told me that her husband's first reaction was to take out more life insurance. He feared that heart trouble might run in the family, and he wanted his wife and children well provided for. Often, however, a heavy load of insurance is part of the chain that drags men into an early grave as they work harder and harder to provide for the future as well as immediate needs.

A pastor mentioned that he has met many widows traveling abroad on their husband's insurance while regretting they never took the trip while their husbands were alive. Some husbands might be better off if they did some traveling together with their wives. It might also be better to give their wives a chance to improve their skills in typing, nursing, or similar occupations, instead of themselves slaving to build up large insurance funds. A wife's best insurance, according to many experts, is a professional degree or some practical training—something that will help her move toward independent living.

At age twenty-two I exchanged my job as a legal secretary for a kitchen sink. I thought I had made an excellent exchange. As a new bride I said goodbye to the world of carbon paper, ledger sheets, typewriter erasers, and coffee breaks, never expecting to return to it. When my husband died sixteen years later and I needed to return to work in order to support my family, society had changed a great deal, but I hadn't. My former skills had rusted from disuse.

The thought of returning to school was most unwelcome. A mother with four children didn't go to school with her daughter! To try to resume an education begun over twenty years ago and kept alive only through general reading seemed a hopeless gesture. Yet early in our marriage our plan had been that after Walter completed his education, I would return to school to complete mine. Returning to these old goals, I began to make arrangements to return to college on a part-time basis.

Any idea I might have had that I was unique in my educational aspirations was soon erased. I discovered that continuing education for the mature student is one of the fastest growing developments in higher education. Everybody was doing it: men, women, beginners in higher education, even Ph.Ds. By far the majority of mature students were women, particularly in the 35 to 45 age bracket. *I* had good reason to go to school. I faced perhaps twenty to thirty years in the labor market to support myself and family. But these others? What were they doing at college? Discovering their reasons for going back to college helped decide my own vocational goals.

I found that the drive of women to get an education was so insistent that universities across the United States were initiating special programs for women in their middle years. Any widow who is considering returning to school should investigate these special programs. One of the main reasons women wanted to continue their education was, of course, to prepare for employment, as I was. A director of the continuing education program at Wichita State University, where I attended, told me that "women see the spiraling cost of living. One salary is simply not enough to cover everything. So women go back to school to update skills that will add a significant second income to the family."

She mentioned another reason not usually stated openly: "Women have come to recognize the tremendous pressures on their husbands to provide for their families. They want to relieve them a bit by supplementing the income."

One man who investigated the cost of life insurance found that his best investment was to give his wife a profession. He sent her off to school so that she could support herself in the event of his death.

But economic pressures aren't the only reason women are returning to school. Many adult students are not financially needy. They come from comfortable, middle-class homes. They are alert, intelligent women who miss the stimulation that college courses can give them. They simply want an opportunity to expand their intellectual interests. The university is there—why not use it to gain an understanding of the modern world's complexity and satisfy a yearning for self-development?

I wanted to provide for myself and the children more adequately than by an office job, and eventually to give myself time for writing. However, my school experience as a mature person also helped me work through the problems of identity created by the death of my husband. I discovered a great deal about myself I never knew existed. I even learned that I enjoyed teaching, a vocation I had sworn as a girl never to enter.

But the transition from housewife to college student has numerous ordeals. Any widow planning to return to school should assess her motivations and abilities realistically, and resolve not to be discouraged at the first setback. Classes demanded far more of me than simply listening to lectures. Being a student required many adjustments, particularly for the family. It meant less time for nonessentials, for general reading, social life, and traveling. I had to struggle with guilt feelings about leaving the children alone several evenings a week. Yet I was pleasantly surprised at the way they enjoyed my new status. They willingly picked up added home responsibilities.

I remember one mother enrolled in an upper division literature course, who emoted poetry to her family at every opportunity. They ate corn flakes to the accompaniment of Shakespearean sonnets. One morning her husband appeared at the breakfast table in his old bathrobe. Usually he came to the table in coat and tie, ready for the office. Eyeing his wife wearily, he asked, "Do I get a clean shirt this morning or more poetry?"

Another widow who had returned to school with some hesitation found university course work so stimulating that she continued until she had completed her degree. One day a friend who couldn't understand her learning aspirations shocked her by saying, "I don't respect you any more."

When I first started back, I was frightened and

insecure. I dreaded the thought of lectures and having to associate with brilliant young college students. I soon found that I could keep up with most students and that most professors enjoyed having adult students in their classes. They liked the contributions we made based on experience. I have since encouraged many widows and other women to return to school, not necessarily for financial rewards, but because of the better contribution they can make to church and society.

Our society has vast reservoirs of intelligent women who have been staffing homes but may now sit idle in empty nests. Many of these women married young; their childbearing years were short. A long stretch of years lies ahead of them with not enough to do.

Most of these women will look for jobs, but may find work that is beneath their real potential. Like myself, they never expected to work outside the home and therefore aren't prepared educationally for challenging jobs. They're often willing to settle for any work that provides an income, that they can do easily, and that fits into their schedule. The peace with vocational mediocrity that comes so easily should be discouraged. Women need to be counseled to begin a personal learning program that will extend for a lifetime. Yet because of financial difficulties, many widows will be unable to enter a formal academic program and may spend years at a job that doesn't make use of their potential.

Some widows who need to return to school in order to provide adequately for their children, may find that the children make it impossible. Nevertheless, when life suddenly loses its center of gravity, every widow faces what to do with her life from here on. The question is hers and hers alone. Most people agree that no decision should be made too quickly. Taking a job may be helpful, but it can't do everything. A job won't cover a widow's grief nor end her loneliness. It can't be the only source of her satisfaction in life, nor will it give her status lost through the death of her husband. Even if she works, there are weekends, vacations, and life's evenings to be taken care of. Loneliness may have to be put out the door every night with the cat.

After Walter's death I found friends pushing me into the traditional role of the widow: "retired from active duty." I'm thankful that God convinced me that if I wanted to remain an authentic individual, the widow's role would be too confining. My husband had always encouraged me in my struggle for self-discovery. It was clear that as a manless woman, with no one to ask what was going on, only faith, courage, determination, and a sense of humor could keep me an informed member of the church. Though forced to return to remunerative work to support my children, I wasn't willing to accept a job as a dead end. I sensed that my widowhood and my vocation were actually of one piece.

I saw two options before me: I could forfeit my life, taking the easy way out by accepting the role the church expected of a woman without a husband—inactive, sub-dued, content with social contacts among other widows. Or I could take my new existence seriously and remain an individual, doing what I thought God wanted of me as a person. I opted for the latter.

I began to redesign and build my life, despite problems of low income, family difficulties, and considerable illness. I thank those friends who encouraged me to return to school to complete a master's degree in English and to begin teaching. I try to view all my experiences as an encounter with God, posing my questions to him and then waiting for him to work it out. Years ago in one of her articles, Dorothy Haskins wrote that she thought widowhood was one of life's three greatest challenges; the other two were conversion and marriage. Widowhood was to her an opportunity to trust God wholly at a time when all earthly props had been pushed out from under her. F. B. Meyer wrote that nothing strengthens a person so much as isolation and transplantation. It forces one to reach out to the sunshine.

How does one prepare for widowhood? A husband can take out a large insurance policy and assure himself that when he dies his wife will be provided for. It would be better if together they make the down payment on a spiritual insurance policy while they are both alive. This involves knowing where one's ultimate security in this life and the life to come lies—in Christ Jesus. Such knowledge helps the surviving spouse to see the past in the right perspective and to see the present with purpose. It also helps one to find the strength to begin the business of living again, not as a former wife, but as a person.

CHAPTER SEVEN
"Lord, I'm So Lonely."

Life, in its greatness and weakness, is a solo, a solitary thing.
—Dr. George Kelsey

"Lord, I'm so lonely tonight. I ache all over. If there's ever a hell on earth, it's this feeling of loneliness, of having been exiled into a never-never land where each day the longing to be close to someone I care about gets stronger. I want to be with a man tonight, Lord, not just by myself. I want to be with just about anybody. I don't want to be alone and lonely.

"The children are all out at their own activities. Here I sit trying to study a Bible lesson for tomorrow's class, and I can't remember from one paragraph to the next what I'm reading. I want the phone to ring, the doorbell to ding-dong. I go to the fridge, look over the half-empty shelves and shut it, knowing that the empty feeling inside isn't hunger but loneliness—the kind food can't satisfy.

"Lord, it's tough being alone. I've got no one to say nice things to me anymore. This afternoon at the faculty meeting I finally dared to give an opinion and the next person swatted it down like a miserable mosquito. I felt pain all over, Lord, not just on one little spot on my arm. I want someone to tell me I'm still worth something—that I count even if my ideas aren't on the same level as Henry Kissinger's.

"I'm lonely, Lord. Don't you hear me? I hurt. I've walked around the block and nothing has changed. I want someone to put his arms around me and say he loves me. I want someone to crawl into bed with me with that eager, happy look.

"I keep remembering, yet I want to forget—the good-bye kiss in the morning that Walter never missed in sixteen years when he was at home. When I crawl into bed alone I think of how I used to put my icy feet—and they were always icy—against his and he never minded a bit. Not once. My sister always used to kick them away when we slept together in the big iron bed upstairs when we were children. Walter sometimes even rubbed my cold feet in his warm hands until I was warm all over.

"I remember how clean he was. How he loved to be neat and clean in body as well as mind and spirit—even his desk—never a paper clip out of place. I wish I could forget, but I can't.

"At coffee break today a group of couples mentioned they were going out for supper tonight. I was there, but no one thought to invite me. I don't fit in. If Walter had been around, we would have been invited. I feel a gulf fixed between me and couples, greater than the one between Lazarus and the rich man. During the day when I'm busy teaching and so forth, it's gone. But then as soon as I move into a social situation, there it is again. At times

I can't stand how much I want to get back into the world of couples.

"The other day I heard that a friend whose husband died only three years ago is getting remarried this summer. I hate the jealous feelings that tear at my heart when I hear such news. I'm glad for her; truly, I am, Lord, but I hate the ugly feelings of self-pity that claim me too.

"Lord, I'm so lonely."

What widow hasn't told the Lord a similar story? Without doubt, the greatest problem she faces is not usually financial, but emotional and spiritual. The cold and terrifying feeling can't be shaken that no one cares whether she gets up in the morning and goes to work, or stays home and does nothing at all. She feels like a plant uprooted from family and friends and thrown off by herself in a lonely corner where love and caring have no room.

A friend once told me of her feeling when, as a refugee in Berlin following World War II, she learned that the rest of her family had been sent back to Russia and she had been stranded alone in the city, a total stranger among the enemy. I tried to empathize with her, but not until Walter's death could I understand what she had been trying to convey. When I too felt like a tiny raft adrift on a great ocean, amid boisterous high waves and no hope of rescue in sight, I understood her plight.

A widow may feel she has a special claim on loneliness because her situation was caused by the death of someone dear to her. Some widows make a specialty of telling everyone about their plight and live unnecessarily lonely lives because they think that this is now their lot. Yet,

I believe, it helps to know that loneliness is a universal feeling. It occurs among the great and the lowly, the rich and the poor, and even among the married, especially those who have the misfortune to have an unhappy re-lationship.

Even Jesus was lonely and longed for the disciples to stay awake and watch with him before the betrayal and crucifixion. The prophet Elijah felt lonely and told the Lord at one point when the wicked queen was chasing him, "It is enough; now, Lord, take my life; for I am no better than my fathers before me"(1 Kings 19:4 NEB). King David, in his flight from Saul, wrote, "I look to my right hand, I find no friend by my side; no way of escape is in sight, no one comes to rescue me" (Psalm 142:4 NEB). The apostle Paul wrote his disciple Timothy that "at the first hearing of my case no one came into court to support me; they all left me in the lurch" (2 Timothy 4:16 NEB).

Loneliness is the common enemy of all humankind, but it may hit widows particularly hard, especially during the first years. Without her life's companion beside her, feeling lonely because she is alone, she may be tempted to tell herself, "No one wants to have anything to do with me anymore. No one loves me." She may withdraw from society even more. Self-abnegation can thus begin so to dominate her life and force her to keep looking at herself instead of out at the world that it may destroy her spirit like a slow-eating cancer.

American author Herman Melville in his short story "Bartleby the Scrivener"pictures a man who in the end is completely alienated from society. The scrivener draws back from everyone in his social environment and from all obligations, step by step, until he dies. His self-alienation finally annihilates him.

Widowhood easily becomes like that. The feeling of worthlessness grows day by day. The desire to be with people diminishes. Meeting the morning becomes a daily agony. Life must be lived, but she'd rather not. A sour, unhappy individual takes over in the widow's home, but she doesn't know it; only the others who watch her know —and wonder how the process can be reversed.

The widow may think she is grieving for her husband, yet if the truth were told, most of us who are widowed grieve for ourselves rather than for the one who died. If we are Christians we know that he has gone to a much better place. But we have been left alone to face the daily miseries of life. We have to eat our unwelcome three meals each day, alone. One widow said she never again ate at the kitchen table where she and her husband had enjoyed so many meals together. After his death, she fixed herself a tray and ate elsewhere in the house, wherever she happened to be working.

We have to do that limp little clump of laundry each week, for ourselves only. We have to pay the bills, go to church, call the plumber, watch the news, alone. We pray alone. We agonize with health alone. We wait out the long evenings alone. One older widow told me she never went out during the evening because she couldn't bear to come to an empty house when she returned. An elderly widower who had known years of happily wedded life suddenly lost his wife through sickness. In the evenings when the shadows darkened and stillness crept over the house, the longing to communicate with someone became so great he simply cried out to the wall.

Emily Carr, Canadian artist, wrote in her journal: "I wonder, will death be much lonelier than life. Life's an awfully lonesome affair. You can live close against other people yet your lives never touch. You come into the world alone and you go out of the world alone, yet it seems to me you are more alone while living than ever going and coming."

If the loneliness is acute and if the widow had a fairly happy mental state before the death of her husband, she may think that remarriage is the answer to her problem. Find a man, quickly, at once. Then the need will be met. So she walks down the street and finds herself examining men. She sits in church, at any kind of meeting, and her eyes drift over the men. She absentmindedly kills off the wife, if there is one, and measures him against her standards—too dominant, too fat, can't use language properly, too sloppy—and then is horrified at her own thoughts and how she has betrayed her own love.

I've read many books on the single life in the last years. Many dwell at length on how to get back into the dating game and secure a husband, or at least how to get sex back into one's life. I believe that many widows would like a second husband, particularly if the first marriage was happy. They enjoy the status of being a wife. The security of a husband to give leadership in the home, to act as an escort, as a companion, and as a lover aren't easily dismissed. Being married is preferable to being single.

Yet most widows have to accept as a realistic fact that they won't marry for the simple reason that there aren't enough men to go around. A newspaper account states that by about 1990 the number of Americans who will have passed their eightieth birthday will treble, and the surplus of elderly widows (over the number of elderly widowers) will grow to eight million. Widows are obviously at a disadvantage in seeking out male company. It's much easier for a widower to find love again than for a widow, especially one with small children. Many a widower with a large family easily finds a woman, single or formerly married, who will accept the responsibility of mothering his family. Yet, strangely, few men who have raised one family will accept the responsibility of raising another man's family. And any widow with small children or teen-agers should recognize that bringing another person into the family may cause added problems, even as it may bring new blessings. Children don't always take kindly to an "intruder" in the family circle. My son looked at me in consternation one day when I jokingly suggested that perhaps I should think of remarrying. Another male in the family? It sounded preposterous.

The widow shouldn't shut out the idea of remarriage, but she should also recognize that it may not happen. Above all, she shouldn't rush it, and especially not decide to get married again before she has found someone willing to marry her.

All of this excellent-sounding advice doesn't answer the question of what she does with her sexual drives if she has been used to regular sexual relationships with her husband. Undoubtedly many widows will be hounded by the idea that sex will satisfy the ache of loneliness. "I feel so lonely. Only when someone is making love to me can I forget how lonely I am," said one single woman.

Dr. David Reed, associate director of the Marriage Council of Philadelphia, refers to the need to be held, to make human contact, as "skin hunger." What widow won't admit to being overcome at times with the longing to be held once again, to have the "skin hunger" satisfied. She longs to enjoy again the little nuances of married life: casual pats and pokes, meaningful glances above the heads of the children, the compliments and jokes, all of which were part of life together. Now they are gone forever, yet they remain one of the needed ingredients of any person's life, married or single, for they are the affirming strokes each person needs to thrive. Where does a widow get this affirmation now?

Many secular books and manuals for the single person openly tell her she is entitled to a social life, and to a sexual life, that she should never feel guilty about making sexual contacts without a commitment of love and marriage. She is advised that no hard and fast rules govern the circumstances under which she should sleep with someone except those that are right for her. She can sleep with anyone she wants to. Her only reason for not doing so should be that she doesn't feel like it. She shouldn't feel she has to "hold out" for a prescribed length of time with any man. Nor should she feel apologetic to the children if they find a strange man sleeping over occasionally. All of this is her right to satisfy her sexual urges.

One author of a book for singles mourns that the biggest problem for former marrieds is that sex becomes unpredictable—it's either a feast or famine, with no insurance that it will be available when most desired. The author expresses surprise that some singles still don't accept sex outside of marriage as their right and privilege. He cautions against mixing sex with other personality stresses. Sex is one function of the personality, love another. Don't mix them or confuse them; it may create a problem.

The thinking behind such advice is that human beings have become fully autonomous creatures who are responsible to no one, not their families, friends, community, or even God. An individual should feel free to develop his or her own standards in matters related to sexual behavior, and it's no one's business except the individuals involved what the extent of the relationship may be.

As a Christian, I cannot accept such advice. I see sex as a function of the total being, a gift from God to enhance and build the marriage relationship, to increase the oneness. It is a way to mutual discovery, for in a sexual encounter one attains a knowledge of the inner secret of the partner's physical being. It is a personal act and a social act that implies consent for all consequences and ramifications. Sexual union without moral union is wrong both before and after marriage, for sex outside of marriage is more than an isolated sexual pleasure. It is an expression of a mental attitude in which God and the other person and self are involved.

Unless a widow is convinced within herself that sex outside of marriage is not for her, she may yield to temptation, concluding that sexual contacts are her right and that it's impossible to live fully without a sex life. Help in solving my own dilemma came when I ran across the statement that the human organism can get along without physical lovemaking (witness the thousands who are sick or in isolated situations who do), but cannot thrive without human affection. A simple statement, but it helped. It was a beginning. I prayed much that my great loneliness would at no point drive me to actions I would later be ashamed of.

The first skirmish in the battle against loneliness is won when the widow can admit her feelings of loneliness and accept responsibility for them. Loneliness is *her* problem, no one else's. Not her dead husband's, nor the neighbor's, nor the deacons', nor her family's. She shouldn't feel guilty about being lonely. The sin comes in letting loneliness paralyze her and turn her into an embittered individual who is useless to herself and to others. She is as responsible to keep loneliness from becoming her keeper as she is to keep the mortgage company from foreclosing. Because she feels lonely when no one is with her, she may think emotional survival depends on a husband or on having other persons nearby much of the time. But the widow who depends on others to meet her emotional needs is deceiving herself.

The next step to victory is to accept solitude as a gift from God. Be thankful for it. I've always been a very private person who can enjoy long periods of solitude. I recommend to any lonely person to consider a prolonged period of being alone as a gift from God for the opportunity to think, to learn to know oneself, and above all to learn to know him better. Begin a serious study of the Bible and of other books. Ponder the purpose of life. As a widow moves more deeply into the truths of the Word of God she will find that her widowhood and the purposes of God for her cannot be separated. They are not separate roles. God will give her special opportunities to serve him and meet the needs of others because she is single. Instead of resenting and resisting solitude, welcome it as a special chance to discover God's leading. A life consisting only of pleasant experiences is seldom conducive to the discovery of meaning. The incentive is lacking when life is wreathed in roses. The apostle Paul, writing to the Philippians, showed that knowing the purpose of life involves effort: "I do not consider myself to have 'arrived,' spiritually, nor do I consider myself already perfect. But I keep going on, grasping ever more firmly that purpose for which Christ Jesus grasped me" (3:13, 14 Phillips).

Consider some of the role models that other widows have left as our example. Paula (347-404) was born into a noble Roman family, so wealthy it owned a whole city. Always interested in religion and education, she devoted herself entirely to charity after her husband's death.

Marcella, another noble and wealthy Roman widow, may have been the first woman to join the Christian monastic movement. Elsie Thomas Culver, in *Women in the World of Religion,* writes that Marcella had been attracted to the ascetic way of life since girlhood. For a period of time the home of her mother became a center for Christian activity and also for a group of women interested in Bible study and church history.

A pioneer in the movement for the education of the child-widows of India in the late 1800s was Pandita Ramabai Sarasvati, herself a widow. She saw the desperate plight of young girls who on the death of their husbands, were forced either to throw themselves upon the funeral pyre or to live a life of shame and misery. Their heads were shaved periodically and they dressed in coarse clothing. In a society handicapped by religious fanaticism and superstition, these child-widows were condemned to a long, poor, friendless widowhood. The story of Ramabai's courageous efforts to provide homes and an education so the girls could become self-supporting is told by Clementina Butler in *Pandita Ramabai Sarasvati.*

Other widows have taken upon themselves the psychological and spiritual counseling of the newly widowed. They find their mandate in Isaiah 61:

> The Spirit of the Lord God is upon me; because the Lord hath anointed me to preach good tidings unto the meek; he hath sent me to bind up the brokenhearted, to proclaim liberty to the captives, and the opening of the prison to them that are bound; To proclaim the acceptable year of the Lord, and the day of vengeance of our God; to comfort all that mourn; to appoint unto them that mourn in Zion, to give unto them beauty for ashes, the oil of joy for mourning, the garment of praise for the spirit of heaviness; that they might be called trees of righteousness . . .

With time their ministry is enlarged to speak to others who have gone through a time of suffering. Together they reaffirm where one's ultimate security rests. They find joy in discovering their gifts and how to minister to others with needs.

In the battle against loneliness, it helps to recognize what triggers the dull ache in the heart, the deserted feeling. "Your song," certain photographs, the knowledge that everyone is going to a party except you, the prospect of an upcoming holiday or vacation and no one to share it with, fatigue and discouragement—all can set off a bout of loneliness. One widow told me that Fridays and Saturdays were the worst, when the children were gone. Another said it was Sundays, the long afternoons and no one to spend them with.

Some of my suggestions may sound harsh, but in the long run they will help. Give away old records and clothes and pieces of furniture to children, relatives, friends, or the Salvation Army if they bring on tears. Don't keep torturing yourself by having reminders of a former life nudging you each day. Be grateful for all good experiences with your husband, but leave them in the past. As soon as I could afford it, I bought myself a single bed, and piece by piece, I got rid of the furniture we had used together, with the exception of a few pieces. In the evening when I go out, I leave a light on so that I come back to warmth and light.

It helps to prepare for weekends and vacations by planning some activity of your own: a shopping trip, a visit, a new book, travel, exercise, a guest over for a meal. Above all, don't let television or its companions in escape artistry—sleep, gossip, drugs, the telephone, or food— become your ersatz companions.

A London woman spent five evenings each week for ten years at the same movie theater, sitting in the same seat. She watched each movie twice. "There's really not very much else to do," said the woman, who lived alone. "Nobody ever visits me, and I hardly know anyone." According to the newspaper story she took an alarm clock set for 8:30 P.M. with her. She liked to get home early so she could rise at an early hour, get her work done, and be fresh for the movies again.

Movies and television are common antidotes for loneliness in America today. The strange phenomenon of our age is that mass communications, which have crowded our world together, at the same time seem to keep people apart, making genuine closeness impossible.

The real cure for loneliness is the healing interaction of two personalities—fellowship. Loneliness leaves when there is sharing of deeper needs, struggles, and joy. People who frequently watch TV or go to movies may almost be convinced that they experience a personal relationship with the people on the screen. This is only a sad illusion. The problem of loneliness is still there when the film has ended. Only the passing of time has occurred. Fellowship was only simulated. And such continual substitutes for two-way communication become a blight upon the personality.

So, recognize the need for human companionship. Friends can bring you courage and hope, which is more necessary to life than happiness. "To live is to love," so don't hole up in your house or apartment. Join clubs, organizations, and activities to the extent that you can enjoy and accommodate these in your schedule. Force yourself to move out of your home at least once each day. If you find yourself enjoying the martyrdom of the lonely widow, give yourself a swift mental kick at regular intervals.

A weekly Bible study group in my community has proven a great help to some widows. Visit the old, the sick, the elderly. Take your neighbor a new dish. Begin a regular correspondence with friends or relatives. Remember that what you do *for* someone helps that person. What you do *with* them helps you both.

If you feel inclined, join a group for singles, of which

many kinds are springing up all over the nation. Be aware, however, that some single groups can be depressing just because they bring together the most lonely people. I remember one meeting for singles I went to at a nearby mental health center. About eighty women had been expected; more than 125 turned up. We had a good time sharing our experiences but even now I remember the compulsive need some had to share the aches in their lives. Talking to them was like being near a gusher.

Don't expect too much of married people, but don't become bitter about it either. Enjoy their friendship when they offer it. Recognize that to the wife you may represent an unconscious threat to the stability of her marriage if her husband pays attention to you. Some will understand. Some won't be as tolerant, but you aren't responsible for their attitudes.

Take time to make friends with individuals who might ordinarily be out of your social group. The Good Samaritan has lived in memory for centuries without a name. The best friends are not always the most important people.

See yourself as a person worthy of love, even if no one at the moment seems to be tripping over his feet with a rose in his teeth to tell you so. As you become more self-sufficient as an uncoupled woman, feelings of inadequacy and loneliness will diminish. Your horizons will expand.

But recognize that loneliness won't disappear overnight. It may have to be swept out with the trash each day. And the problem may return bigger than ever when you're faced with a big decision like a job change or a crisis with a child. When the thought comes over you of the grandchild who never knows a grandfather's love, the son who never experiences a father's praise, the daughter who never has the strong arm of an older man around her shoulders, take a few minutes to weep. But only a few minutes. Then get on with living once again.

And in living, hang onto Christ as Lord and Savior. He can be your personal friend. I know that many people (myself included) whose religious experience has been mostly a little upheaval now and then, wish desperately for some way of damming up the Holy Spirit in a person's life. Then they might come through with a whopper of a spiritual experience once in awhile not just to have something to say at a testimony meeting, but because God would thereby become a real person to them. Then they could face any trial, including widowhood.

Most Christians have been taught from childhood that God is a person and can be known as a person. Yet what does the preacher mean when he says that a Christian can have a personal relationship with God?

According to A. W. Tozer, for most non-Christians God is nothing more than an inference or a deduction. They may think of him as an ideal or as a symbol of goodness, beauty, truth, or love. But even though most Christians would agree that God has a personality and can be known as a person, Tozer thinks that God is no more real to them than he is to the non-Christian. A "personal relationship" with Jesus Christ is something they'd like to have, but they don't know what to do to make Christ real to them.

I'm glad that the reality of God doesn't depend on what I believe. God has existence as a Spirit endowed with a personality apart from anything I choose to believe about him. The Bible says so. I'm glad that God can be known by human beings. Again, the Bible says so. "They that seek me, shall find me."

If it's possible to know God, then we must have faculties suited for that purpose. These faculties, though seldom used, are spiritual and are brought to life through the new birth. "He that cometh to God must believe that he is, and that he is a rewarder of them that diligently seek him" (Hebrews 11:6).

How do I know that God is real? I can't see him. I can't reach out and touch him with my hands. I can't hear an audible voice. No, I may not be able to do these things, but I know him because he has given me an inner consciousness of himself. I hear his voice speaking to my spirit when I become quiet and listen. I feel the strength of his arms supporting me the way a father carries a weary child. The reality of Christ is grasped by the soul. It requires the leap of faith.

If our search is for the experience itself, we will miss both it and Christ. If we are after God, we shall have all we need. The widow can with great boldness say with the apostle Paul, "For I am persuaded, that neither death, nor life, nor angels, nor principalities, nor powers, nor things present, nor things to come, nor height, nor depth, nor any other creature, shall be able to separate us from the love of God, which is in Christ Jesus our Lord" (Romans 8:38, 39).

CHAPTER EIGHT
Parent without Partner

What is a man's first duty to his children? It is most important to provide support, loving companionship, spiritual training, discipline, education. But there is another duty that must come first. It is the duty to make the children's mother happy. —Concord Associates*

"I want you at home! I don't want to be baby-sitted!"

I tried to erase these words and the vision of my little boy's tear-stained face from my mind as I drove away from the baby-sitter's home to go to work. But what could I do?

A good, responsible person was taking care of him, but four-year-old Jamie wanted things to be the way they were before. A few months ago, when his mother was at home each day taking care of him, there had been time for games and stories and walks together.

I wondered how other widows had solved this problem when they had to work. Most run-of-the-mill books on

*Found in Walter's Bible after his death.

child training don't treat the matter of one-parent homes. They're not written for families where the father is absent because of separation, desertion, divorce, or imprisonment—or for more respectable reasons such as lengthy hospitalization, out-of-town employment, or death.

Any time a home is broken, pain is present. Humiliation is added to the hurt when the cause of the break is not socially acceptable. Sometimes when selfishness and neglect have been major factors in the parents' failure, the one trying to carry on alone may feel that no help from human beings or God should be expected.

My husband died a respectable death because of a chronic disease, but even so it was hard for me to find help. I was overwhelmed at times by the painful reality. His place at the table was empty. I was now the bread-winner and sole parent of four lively children.

Now, however, we were experiencing another loss as a family, much more subtle in its invasion of our home than death had been. Touch, sight, hearing, smell—all were useless to indicate to me what had left us. Yet each evening as I entered the door to face the evening's schedule of housework, I knew something was missing.

As we sat at supper one evening a few months after Walter's death, I was sensing the lack. It wasn't the food; the girls were becoming fairly good cooks. The little dining area where we ate was crowded by five people, but it felt empty. At that moment God made me aware of what was missing. The family feeling was gone, that feeling of contented oneness and belonging. Death had robbed us of one parent, and now it was threatening to break up the whole family. We were becoming a group of five people living together in one house, one very busy woman and four children of assorted ages coming together to eat and to sleep. In trying so hard to earn shoes and bread for five, I had forgotten that life is more than a new dress for the spring concert or fried chicken for Sunday dinner.

When the family feeling is gone, how does one bring it back?

The way a family copes with its problems is the measure of its strength. One evening, problems seemed to have battered our family's stress tolerance to the limit. Tears, anger, and hard words had been tossed about like confetti at a wedding. I knew that something had to be done. I sat down at my desk to identify my biggest problems, jotting them down on a scrap of paper so I could look at them objectively. I began with the most acute ones. I have added others mentally since that evening (new ones always come up as family circumstances change). I know I cannot expect life to move on without some stumbling. Even complete families cannot expect that. It isn't the problems, but what we do with them that's important.

My list looked something like this:

1. How to keep the morning exodus from being a free-for-all rat race.

2. How to keep that family feeling in the confusion of the evening return.

3. How to find more time for making meals, laundry, and housekeeping jobs.

4. How to help the children feel more secure.

5. How to keep the masculine element in the children's lives.

Just holding each problem at arm's length helped me tremendously, and I felt vastly better when I went to bed that evening. I now had a goal and a plan.

The morning getaway was our bugaboo. Although it improved much after this, I don't think we ever achieved a really graceful exit while the children were young. Trying to get myself and also the children ready for the day always seemed to end in a snarl somewhere with a sock or a book misplaced, and everyone being pressed into service to find the missing item.

Part of my new plan was to start the morning preparations the night before by helping the children get their clothes ready, having breakfast partly laid out, and meals planned for the day. I also pinned up lists telling each child her tasks for the day. A little black-covered notebook became our daily log. I've noticed how even now the older girls sometimes return to this little book for recipes one doesn't find in cookbooks, for in it I gave instructions about exact times to put various foods on the stove and what kinds of saucepans to use.

> Add 1½ cups diced potatoes to soup at 4 o'clock and 3 tblsp. rice. Make sure it starts boiling again.
> There are two containers of mashed potatoes in fridge. Heat slowly in a heavy, covered saucepan. Macaroni and cheese at 4:30 at 350°. Watch it!
> I will make gravy when I get home.
> Get Chris to bring in laundry. Clean up clothes NEATLY upstairs.
> Do some ironing. Watch synthetics. Put out garbage.
> Clean out all cat's mess in basement.

The other part of my plan was to get to bed earlier and to get up earlier, for most tensions can be greatly eased by getting more sleep. Early to bed is a habit I've maintained throughout graduate school to the present. The earlier rising hour avoided that headlong rush into the day's activities, which causes feelings of busyness and stress to multiply as the minutes hurtle along. Earlier rising, though difficult at first, gave me the opportunity for at least a few quiet moments before the children began bombarding me with their requests for advice and help.

Most working mothers experience some of the same early-morning problems. Little children have to be ready to leave the house when Mother goes; so instead of patiently waiting for them to tug on little shoes and socks, Mother hastily scoops up the child and pulls on the awkward garments. Nor is there time for the child to eat at his own slow pace. Before long the child waits to be dressed and fed each morning.

An earlier rising bell helped a lot. It was better to have five minutes to spare and be able to leave the house calm and at ease than to rush out the door still urging the late ones to hurry and reminding the others of forgotten tasks while putting on my own shoes and coat.

The evening return was harder to unkink. The children usually came home before I did, with one of the older girls stopping off at the babysitter to pick up Jamie. They all had some small tasks to attend to before I arrived home. But usually the moment I entered the door, at least one was waiting to nab my attention to tell me about a grade, the need for 75 cents for a book, or a party at church. I was tired from a day's work; we were all hungry, and sometimes someone had to run to the store to get something needed for our evening meal. The child who dared to move in and ask when angels fear to tread usually had little success. Although it may not have been the best procedure I tried to convince the children to hold their requests at least ten minutes before they bombarded me with anything requiring a decision on my part. The older girls began coaching the younger ones to wait for the "right psychological moment" to make their demands. Even now we joke about five o'clock not being the right psychological moment to make requests of Mother to use the car or similar matters. Wait until Mother has taken her shoes off.

The first year in Hillsboro we received many callers who were interested in our welfare. I appreciated the kindness of the Christians in this small town who sincerely helped as they were able, but I often wished they would visit us at hours that suited the needs of my family rather than their own. Visitors usually came at the time I was about to bathe and put the younger children to bed, so Jamie squirmed and fussed while I tried to make small talk with visitors. My suggestion to widows in similar situations is to ask friends to come later, say at 9:30 or 10:00 P.M. when the children are in bed. Then they will be free to enjoy having someone to converse with over a cup of coffee.

The secret of success for any family is a tie of some kind which holds the individual members together even when the family is apart, but this can't be pushed on a family. In school a teacher says, "Today we will have a lesson in spelling," and the children are expected to learn twenty words. In the home it doesn't work that way. You can't decide that today you'll teach the children love, and tomorrow you'll give them a lesson in forgiveness. These are byproducts of living. A child learns that God forgives if he has already learned that parents forgive.

I learned love one unhappy Christmas at about the age of ten or eleven when I was sick with the measles—red, feverish and desperately uncomfortable with the itching and the coughing. Mother loved me enough to leave her bed and sleep with her miserable child. I never consciously knew that I was learning lessons of security and hope and understanding as a child, but knew how good it felt to gather around the oil-cloth-covered table beneath the kerosene lamp and eat our evening meal together. Father was home from work; we were together. The world was shut out for a little while, and love was shut in.

I recall the long drive home after a day of attending church and visiting friends in the community twenty miles from where we lived. Cold, sleepy, and cross with one another because all five of us children couldn't lie down in the back seat of our 1932 model car, we still knew we were going home. My parents were never able to give us much money or many clothes, but in many ways they gave us more important things—a sense of personal worth before God and man, courage, hope, and love for one another. Our feeling of oneness was usually centered in some joint activity of all members of the family.

Now as a single parent, I realized that my own children needed more joint activities to bond us together. We found one in the family devotional period we tried to hold after the evening meal. Daddy was no longer a physical presence. By continuing our "family altar" as we had done before he left us, we discovered what God, our heavenly Father, might mean for a fatherless family.

God has special promises for such families. We claimed them for ourselves.

We began to pray about specific problems, such as what to do when schedules got fouled up or when there wasn't time to do the laundry, or—our biggest specter— what to do when one of the children got sick, with no relative closer than 1,500 miles. As we reached out in faith to God, he met our need. One day Christine got stomach flu at school, so the teacher took her to her home for the rest of the afternoon. I faced the problem of what to do the next few days until she was completely well. Then 76-year-old Grandma Hiebert, our cheerful neighbor, dropped in, and seeing the problem, offered to take care of her. So Chris lay on Grandma Hiebert's davenport and kept her company for the next two days.

Our house seemed to have been built for the tropics instead of the Kansas winter. Once I happened to mention at the office that the children had all complained of being too cold the night before. I had to give them each a sleeping bag to keep warm in. The wife of another employee brought us a thick woolen blanket and some quilts being discarded because her family had switched to electric blankets. Our needs were continually met in such ways. As others opened their hearts to me, I learned one thing: I have never loved enough.

Most working mothers have only limited time with their children; if they want that time to count, they have to make wise use of those few hours. Letting non-essentials in housework go was difficult for me at first, for I had always been a neat, fastidious housekeeper. Yet I realized that time spent talking with the older girls or playing with the younger children was more important.

Whereas I had hated toy-strewn rooms, now I learned to step over blocks, trikes, and trucks. Talking after the supper meal sometimes stretched out longer than we planned. "Let's talk some more," Christine would say, as we discussed, reminisced, or philosophized. Of course, if we talked, the dishes were postponed so much longer.

Shopping for groceries became a once-a-week affair. I had no scruples about TV dinners, pot pies, cake mixes, or other kinds of ready-to-eat foods. I thanked God for every convenience food. I limited ironing strictly to items of clothing like shirts and blouses, and streamlined other housekeeping tasks to meet only the basic requirements of health, comfort, and convenience. I saw no point in trying to be a Superwoman who did everything like the lady on the hill with a maid and butler.

Trying to keep a masculine element in the children's lives is, of course, very difficult. "Aren't we ever going to invite anyone with a daddy anymore?" asked one of the children after several Sundays of just lady visitors. The social life of an incomplete family will always remain one of its most difficult problems in a society geared to couples and complete families. We have found no satisfactory answer to the matter of "Let's go visiting." We have often been lonely. But we have gone picnicking, hiking, and sightseeing in the area. We have visited all the cemeteries and tried to figure out who was related to whom. One summer before a church centennial celebration, we visited old historical sites, including an orphans' graveyard.

Being without a father made the younger children interesting personalities among their friends. On Father's Day when the other children made gifts for their fathers, my son made one for his mother. Other little boys and girls couldn't understand why he didn't have a daddy.

Again and again he came home with questions. Hard ones, too. Why don't I have a daddy anymore? Where is Daddy now? Why didn't God make him well? Will we see him again? If he's in heaven, why doesn't he need his bones in the grave? How will we know him in heaven without his bones and his clothes?

To understand death, children need to experience life. They find it difficult to accept the incomplete end of anything. One of my biggest challenges is transferring the hope of the resurrection in Christ Jesus to the children. I pray that they may have the confidence to believe that even in death there is hope and that in life there must always be courage.

A family is also built into a strong unit by the members working cooperatively together. When one member is missing, the others have to do a little extra. It hurt me to see my youngsters struggling with adult-sized jobs and problems, but I was encouraged when I recognized in the older ones a growing sense of responsibility and care for the younger children.

As a working mother, I found that I was sometimes tempted to take advantage of a conscientious child's sense of duty and overburden her before she was ready for so much responsibility. The spirits of the children can also be blighted by too great an awareness of some of the problems that belong in the adult world—finances, for example.

During one difficult period when we pinched pennies harder than usual, the children became too conscious of financial pressure. I sensed it bearing down on them.

Spirits were heavy. "We can't do anything. We can't buy anything. We can't afford anything." Mother had become a Scrooge.

Widows who must manage family finances alone for the first time without the security of a husband's income will find themselves being overly cautious. I was. I feared pauperdom as much as illness. As I learned to trust God in such matters, the children also came through with a more cheerful outlook. "Maybe we can't take that trip this summer, but we can do some other things."

On the other hand, a widow's love for her children may tempt her to shield them from hard experiences in life. "I had a hard struggle," said one parent, "and I don't want my children to go through such experiences if I can help it." So her child never learned to make his own bed or polish his own shoes. In later years every decision, regardless of how small, upset him.

Children need the experience of deciding certain crucial issues for themselves. This is hard for any parents, but especially for a widow. She may think the child has enough to bear not having a father, without adding other problems to his life. So she takes over for him.

With the father gone there may also be a temptation to let things go: house, car, lawn. The sense of pride in ownership is gone because the one who found joy in keeping the house and yard in good repair is no longer there. It's important to wash and wax the car, to clip the hedges, to keep the house tidy, to keep oneself neatly groomed and attractive, and to keep the children happy.

Fear of inanimate things bothers many women who live alone as much as giant problems in the spiritual realm. We believe that God answers prayers for courage, for strength, and for joy, but what can he do for leaky faucets and broken bicycles? I've shed many tears of frustration and agony over my children's behavior and my own lack of courage and peace of mind. I've shed even more over doors that won't close, drains that won't drain, and furnaces that refuse to heat.

The first summer after Walter's death, whenever I turned a corner the car made the oddest bumping sound. I was terrified. Immediately I envisioned the worst. I would drive a few blocks, turn a corner, and—bop-bop-bop—the noise re-appeared. It seemed even worse than before. Bills, more bills. I could hardly sleep that night.

The next day I had the sense to look under the car; it would have been even more sensible simply to take the car to a garage. I hadn't learned that approach yet, possibly because I was afraid of what the mechanic might say. I didn't know what I expected to see, because I didn't know what the bottom of a car looked like, but I did see something (a loose muffler). My spiritual recovery was immediate. One dollar and sixty-five cents and the help of a friend fixed it.

I've learned since that most things that are broken can be fixed. Skilled mechanics and craftsmen are available for such tasks if I can't tackle them alone. Further, most men are considerate of such problems. As women, we waste too much nervous energy on inanimate objects. A short course in mechanics or plumbing might dry up many tears.

As the children moved through grade school, high school, and now college, I believe we managed to hang onto the idea that we are a family. Something holds us together. Our family hasn't been spared many of the problems that afflict complete families today: illness, college finances, the generation gap, counter-culture ideas, vocational problems, women's liberation, opposition to the institution of the church, and so on. In certain areas of our relationships, unsolved problems remain. Sometimes we drag along for weeks and months with no noticeable progress, and then along comes an incident to show we're learning.

The fall leaves had been dropping for several weeks, heavily covering the lawn. One day I laid down an ultimatum that that evening everyone would rake leaves. No one would get an exemption from work for any reason.

Shortly after supper the rakes came out and the work began. One child grumbled because she couldn't stay in and read her library book. Another didn't see why we couldn't just let the wind get rid of the leaves. But I persisted, and we worked together.

When the big pile of leaves was burning, the children warmed to the situation. They brought out foil-wrapped apples and buried them in the fire.

Late that evening as the fire embers flickered in the darkness, we sat together on the back step, tired and dirty, eating ice cream and discussing the relative merits of half-baked apples. A hush fell on us as we huddled together and enjoyed the gradually encroaching night. The grumbling was gone. In its place were a happy silence and the good feeling that "we're still a family."

I knew then that we were winning.

CHAPTER NINE
"Thanks, You Helped Me."

"And one of them . . . turned back, and with a loud voice glorified God, and fell down on his face at his feet, giving him thanks" (Luke 17:15, 16).

"I never go anywhere. I just stay at home and take care of the kids."

Her husband had died two years ago leaving her with three small children under the age of five. Sitting on my living room couch, her dark eyes looking straight at me, she made the comment without much emotion. That was simply the way it was. Her life had become the care and keeping of three small children because there was no one else to help.

A group of parents without partners had gathered at my house for a discussion of their needs and problems and to probe whether they could form an organization. Because my own four children are nearly all through the adolescent wilderness, my own needs seemed trivial as I listened to these younger mothers with toddlers and grade school children discuss their situation.

Behind their words I read the message I had so often asked myself, "Who will help me raise my family into loving, responsible citizens? Do I have to do it all alone?" In a one-parent family, the lessons in living that are needed to survive seem too many to be taught by only one person, hindered as she may be at times by her own emotional upheavals and spiritual dearth.

Do I have to do it alone? I hadn't, I reflected. Living in a community characterized by care and concern, and being part of a church that tried to see needs as they came up, I had enjoyed the help of many people in "bringing up my children." A few had been willing to be that out-side-the-home adult willing to listen to them and to me. Others had been perceptive people who saw needs that my myopic vision, directed mostly to providing basic necessities, didn't see.

Single-parent families survive well only with support and caring from others, I concluded, as I listened to these women discuss their needs. Where had my support come from? Later I took out a piece of paper and pencil and began listing incidents. I talked to some of the children and asked for their views. Before long we realized we hadn't said thank-you often enough in the years since Walter's death.

Nothing helps the readjustment and rehabilitation of widowed persons as much as solid, long-range support. We were complete strangers in the community in which my husband died only two months after we had moved there. "Give us your burden," said new-found friends. Some are still bearing it now.

During the early years, one evening as we approached the home of friends to eat our evening meal with them,

James, then age four, recognized a car in their driveway. "They still got their grandpas with them," he shouted gleefully. To him, grandparents had only one gender, but he knew David and Nathan always shared the teasing and tussling of Grandpa Faul with him.

One older man took time to swing Jamie gleefully over his shoulder and stuff his pockets with candy each time he saw him. His wife became grandmother to the girls and a friend to me. An older woman picked up the laundry each week for several months, slipped it back into the house again beautifully folded and ironed, and said, "I am doing this for my Lord. I will not take any money from you."

How do you say thanks to the missionary, now returned to the field, who would fix our balky furnace or lawn mower when the conversation between his wife and me drifted too much into woman's talk? When that family left our area, we missed them very much. Their four children matched mine in interests and outlook. Gretchen had the knack of finding laughter when I was holding back tears. My Susan suggested that we get a tape recording of Gretchen's laugh to give us a boost when we were feeling sad. How I appreciated it when their evening walk brought George and Gretchen to our house late enough for a short chat after the children were asleep.

Grandparents of other children stretched their arms wide enough to bring my youngsters into another family circle. Recently, my two youngest children planned to go fishing. The creek runs through the farm of an elderly couple. Should they phone they were coming ? No, the invitation to fish there is like open season on pheasants the year round. Both Christine, 19, and James, 15, knew it was probably their last outing together before she left for her summer job. With fishing rods, sweaters, and a thermos of hot chocolate, they drove off in the early evening. When they hadn't returned by 10:30 P.M., I had a fairly good idea what might have happened. But I phoned to the farm anyway to find out what had happened to my eager anglers.

Mr. John B. Jost, a man in his late sixties, laughed when I phoned. He had expected the call. The children were on their way home, he said. A few minutes later they came bouncing into the house with four catfish. The evening had turned out as they had secretly hoped it would. When they arrived at the farmyard to dig worms, Mr. Jost had joined their fishing expedition to the creek. Later Mrs. Jost had invited them in for an evening snack. The hot chocolate was merely token insurance for the bigger lunch they had confidence would be forthcoming once the Josts knew they were around.

When younger, the children spent frequent weekends at the farm just like the Josts' own grandchildren. Christine, my third daughter, who at home always had to share a room with her sisters, became a princess for a night with a room of her own when she walked up the stairs at the farm. Mrs. Jost still smiles at the first time Chris, then in grade school, lowered herself into the bed and murmured, "What luxury." So little to give a child, and yet so much.

Chris recalls one evening when she and a friend biked out to the farm—for the ride, they said. After a little visiting with the Josts, it was obviously too dark to ride back into town. Mrs. Jost invited them to sleep there. "We planned it that way," Chris says now.

James used similar tactics to wheedle a little time and love for himself. Loaded with lunch and fishing gear, he often biked out to the farm to spend the day at the creek. He seldom caught many fish, but it became a family joke that though he always ate the food he brought along, he usually joined the Josts for their evening meal a little later and could see nothing incongruous about such an arrangement. Why turn down a good meal and fellowship with friends?

Unmerited love abounded at all seasons. The summer of the space ship stands out in my mind. First was born in Jamie's mind the unprecedented idea of building his own model space ship. For several days the idea incubated in his seven-year-old head with occasional mutterings to the rest of the family about this scientific wonder he was planning to make. Sketches were penciled on paper. Then came a period of salvaging building materials, mostly tin cans. It was a period of repeated frustration for him when forgetful sisters and I kept dumping his cans into the garbage.

When he had finally collected enough cans, the moment had arrived for blueprints to become reality. This was, however, also the moment of deepest despair. I, chief assistant engineer, was too ignorant of space ships to be helpful. Nor did I know enough about using tools. A project capable of changing the course of scientific history seemed doomed to permanent failure; humankind might never know another Sputnik.

Somehow Jamie's plight came to the attention of Mr. Jost. He took Jamie with him to his workshop on the farm and helped him put together that vital building material into a wondrous conglomeration of solder and tin. The happiest boy in the world came home that evening because an older man had helped with an act of creation. Can such love be measured or even thanked?

Other "grandpas" of both genders also gave us support. For ten years Mr. and Mrs. P. B. Willems lived close enough for easy shouting across the back yard. "Come over for ice cream and cookies" was a frequent message in the early evening. "Mr. Willems is going to cook dinner today" meant an invitation to eat with them at the Ramada Inn, a rare treat for a low-budget family that hadn't yet graduated from McDonalds. Their fridge was always supplied with pop for little boys who were suddenly thirsty.

Mr. and Mrs. Willems in their simple white house across the tracks provided much needed security for all of us for many years. The children had someone to turn to at any time when I was at work or elsewhere. I had someone to talk to after the children were in bed. I love my children and enjoy being with them, but as a widow I especially longed for someone to discuss adult subjects of interest to me.

Christmas, a bittersweet time for any one-parent family, and particularly for a family living so far from relatives, always meant we temporarily became part of the Willems' clan. We weren't the only strangers at the gate who sat around their dinner table at that time.

After the dishes had been washed, we chatted or played games while the children scooted around making noise. How I was reminded of my own childhood and my own father when Mr. Willems handed everyone a bag of Christmas candy and nuts and then passed out chocolate bars and finally huge oranges. We didn't need the food, but we did need the love.

After Mr. and Mrs. Willems moved to another part of town, I missed being able to say to the children if I had to be away, "Call the Willemses if you don't know what to do." But even now they're not too far away to help. Recently I had to attend an overnight meeting in a distant part of the state. I arranged with James, the only child at home, either to ask his friend to spend the night with him, or if absolutely necessary, to ask the Willemses if he could sleep at their place. The next day when I returned I asked him what he had done. He hadn't bothered asking his friend to come over. Eating supper and sleeping in the spare bedroom in the Willemses' apartment sounded more appealing, so he had gone there. And he had been welcomed.

The children's own grandparents have always lived several thousand miles away, yet seemed close. Grandma's regular gifts of "big" pyjamas ("They'll grow into them") will be missed now that she can no longer do as much sewing. The birthday dollars, even for the older children, always mean love coming from a distance. Grandpa's constant praise and support in his letters and the relaxed caring of both grandparents when we do visit them have helped the children to see themselves as worthwhile persons. "Grandpa and Grandma really like us."

Civic organizations such as Boy Scouts and Girl Guides offer helpful support. But outstanding in my mind is a whole series of Big Brothers who have been involved in our family, primarily with James, through a social work program of the local college. They provided masculine activities, talk, and viewpoints. For several seasons, weekend campouts were a regular feature. College students Paul and Harley packed up a group of boys and their sleeping bags for an overnight at the nearby reservoir. Systematic mother-type packing may have been missing, but the boys enjoyed their outings even when snow frosted their sleeping bags or when someone forgot the butter so that the fried eggs stuck to the pan at breakfast-time.

Equally exciting to James were opportunities to spend a night in the men's dormitory at the college and go out for pizza at midnight. Once these Big Brothers took the boys "snipe hunting." Even the local policeman didn't enlighten the ignorant hunters when he stopped to find out what they were doing whistling to the wind and waiting in the darkness with open paper sacks.

James reported one day that some boys with fathers were jealous of his Big Brother, who involved him in so much fun. It seemed a strange reversal of roles to him. Though some relationships with these young men worked out better than others, I have watched a remarkable, enduring friendship being welded between a young boy and a college student.

"When I have something on my mind, I can go talk it over with Tim," James once explained. God and girls, flying and computers, school and sisters. All need a sounding board.

When James heard that Harley was leaving for voluntary service overseas after graduation from college, his eyes filled with tears. I was sorry with him. Harley had been a special friend to him. Though some people may think the younger generation is moving downhill, I have enough personal experience to know many who are going the other direction.

Possibly because they were older, James' sisters had already learned to expect their main support from within the family before their father's death. But there were many who helped all the children: a friend who provided a party dress for a special banquet; an aunt (who always does everything with a flourish) who provided happy moments with big straw hats decorated with loads of plastic fruit and flowers to parade around in one summer; another aunt who taught Susan how to sew; a teacher who shares James' present model airplane interest; another teacher who has helped him track down international radio stations on short wave; the friend who knew Chris wanted doll clothes and brought some over one evening complete with canopied bed for her Tammy doll. And it wasn't even her birthday.

"Why did all of these people do this?" I asked James one evening. He has fished, hunted, camped, eaten pancake breakfasts and chicken suppers, played and laughed with so many friends outside the family. He has also sat and cried and bemoaned his lot for long afternoons, wishing someone would notice him and take him fishing or do something with him. So many had promised at some visit to do so. He couldn't understand empty promises. *He* always remembered.

"I don't think Mr. Jost does it because he feels he has to —because it says in the Bible to help the widows and the orphans and all that." He fumbled for words. "I think he does it because he likes us." He had already sensed the oughtness that sometimes accompanies charity. He didn't like that kind. Yet which kind is really Christian love?

Whatever the reason behind the caring, the love we have experienced has taught the children to love. Mrs. Jost, our older friend, had been critically ill for several months. When she returned home from her long stay in the hospital, we went to see her. Without prompting, James put his young arms around her thin shoulders and kissed her gently. I knew then he liked her too.

The year of the fishing trip with James, Chris wrote back from her summer job about that last spring outing. "As Mr. Jost, James, and I rode back to the farmhouse that evening, the lights of the pickup truck cut before us in the dark. Shorty, the dog, bounded ahead of us in the light. It was a warm moment that was sad because I knew that the feeling of togetherness couldn't last."

Two young people and an older man in the cab of a farm truck. Togetherness. Fall would bring changes. The Josts were planning to move to town and retire. Chris's activities too would change.

As I read her letter I thought again of the young woman with her three small children from the neighboring community. Who would help her bring up her children as others had helped me? Social workers? Official deacon visits? Other agencies? Can a structured and organized type of love do the job?

Each fatherless family at some point begins to dream again and make plans for the future, but fears often stay with them, at times drowning out the hopes. Such families need encouragement every step of the way. They need friends they can love and trust to reassure them they are on the right track.

142

CHAPTER TEN
When God Does Not Heal

> *Earthquakes do not scorn*
> *The just man to entomb,*
> *Nor lightning stand aside*
> *To find his virtues room.*
>
> —Matthew Arnold

The husband of a friend had been seriously ill for some time. The best available medical attention hadn't helped him. The disease was one still considered beyond the skill of doctors.

In keeping with the scriptural injunction in James 5, the family called the minister and deacons of the church, who anointed the sick man with oil and prayed for his healing. A week later he died.

I listened quietly to comments that slid into the conversation after the funeral as friends and acquaintances discussed the man's untimely death. In his early forties, he left a wife, three young children, and the promise of a fruitful pastoral ministry. Some wondered skeptically what kind of Pollyanna faith would deny the realities of life and expect God to heal a disease for which the medical profession had no cure. Wasn't it rather ridiculous to have a healing service for him? Others wondered more kindly yet with obvious bewilderment: when people pray in faith and God doesn't heal, is that faith vain? Is the death of a loved one the reward for putting one's faith in God? How does one calm the questioning within one's own spirit after such a disappointing experience? Can God heal today as he did centuries ago when the blind and the lame who came to Christ were restored to wholeness? Can we believe everything in the New Testament, especially the wonderful promises about asking anything in his name, knowing that God will hear? Can we apply the words of the New Testament to today's situations?

Renewed interest in spiritual healing of physical ailments is offering hundreds of sick people hope of recovery. The healing movement is gaining impetus among established churches and shedding its attachment to quackery. Some leaders believe that healing is one of the long-neglected ministries of the church and should not be relegated to a specific dispensation, for example, the times of the apostles. Lack of nurture of this gift represents a failure on the part of the church, according to them; its emergence, a return to faithfulness to God's truths.

Though some give wholehearted assent to a healing ministry, other Christians walk around it like last week's garbage or a dog with mange. They fear that any contact with it may taint them with fanaticism, a characteristic of some of the cults that have dabbled in faith healing. They want to avoid identification with the false promises and hopes of "faith healers." As one person said, faith healing seems too much like "pointing a pistol at God while demanding his wonder-working power."

There is undeniably a resurgence of interest in the charismatic movement with its emphasis on gifts, including the gift of healing, as well as in occult and psychic phenomena. Many individuals are beginning to investigate faith healing, some wholeheartedly, others with the hesitance of someone skinny-dipping in the creek on a nippy spring day.

Some try spiritual healing, don't like it or its results, and move to other resources for help. Others end up disillusioned. They have traveled long distances to healing meetings, sat under the ministry of one healer after another, read all the literature, worked up a sweat in prayer, listened to the pounding of their hearts time after time while wondering if it might not be their turn to bathe in the pool of Siloam. They have craved to experience the tingling power of healing flowing through their bodies, yet have come home to watch their disease progress. They haven't discovered the magic formula for healing. Why can't they learn the right words? What has God got against them? Why doesn't God come to their rescue? Their anguish is pathetic.

I have long agreed with the late V. Raymond Edman, who wrote in *Out of My Life,* that certain spiritual experiences should remain a secret between the believer and his Lord and need not be blurted out at some public gathering on demand. Though listeners may enjoy a vicarious thrill by listening to a widow's story of intense longing for healing for her husband's sickness, of darkness and suffering during a long illness, unless the entire testimony is prompted by the Spirit to glorify God, it may do less good than listening to a daytime soap opera.

For years I hugged to myself my deep feelings about my husband's illness and death. Some experiences were too personal and too precious to share in wholesale fashion; others confused and perplexed me. The perspective of time brought greater understanding of what had taken place. Realization that my experience was not unique has given me freedom to speak and write about it. Sharing my perceptions might make the darkness less dense for other widows. If someone had shared more of their confusion and hurt with me, it might not have made the sorrow less, but it would have assured me that the long night was not eternal.

After my husband's first illness in the fall of 1958, we lived with sickness for the next four years, punctuated with both long and short periods of good health. Walter had always been a serious Bible scholar from the time of his conversion at seventeen. He determined to serve God when he stepped out of his old gang gathered at the local revival meetings to make fun of those who went forward. Most of those young men were high school dropouts and life dropouts. During the Depression it was common for young and old to "sit out life" in front of the stores on Main Street, inside pool halls, or walking the streets. Others watched the struggle for real life from the balcony or the back row in church sanctuaries.

Walter made a clean break with his old friends, and returned to high school, from which he had flunked out in ninth grade, to become an honors student. His early journals show always one goal: to know and do the will of God. His early Bible knowledge came mostly through self-teaching, for he spent four years in an alternative service assignment in a lumber camp during World War II as a conscientious objector. During the long winter evenings he and his friends conducted Bible studies among themselves. He often tried fasting for greater spiritual discernment. He kept many notes of his Bible study and continued this practice after we were married, as he was able. I often found him reading his Bible at odd moments of the day. He also made it a practice to write out at length any important decisions before him, listing on paper what he saw as the signposts of God's direction. When doubts came, he could go back to test his earlier thinking.

When he first became ill, we were driven to God's Word, and to prayer. It seemed logical and natural to do what we had been in the habit of doing: telling God about our needs. We spent much time searching the Word of God. We were in need—great physical need and deeper spiritual need, as those who are sick or who have a sick family member will understand. Few young husbands want to die. Few young wives want to give up their husbands so soon. Walter was forty when he first became ill; I was six years younger. Death doesn't seem like part of the plan when living is on the docket.

As we read the Gospels together, we noticed how Christ was always concerned with the whole man as he ministered to the people. He had great compassion for the physical and spiritual needs of people. He healed blind Bartimaeus and the ten lepers. He cast out devils. He restored to life the son of the widow of Nain and also Jairus's daughter. Before he sent his disciples out, he instructed them "to preach the kingdom of God, and to heal the sick"(Luke 9:2). He used many different means

147

for this healing: spittle, clay, hands, washing, bathing. No one pattern of healing prevailed in his ministry.

We studied together the Acts of the Apostles and other portions of the New Testament. We saw that healing had also been an integral part of the ministry of the early church. A forty-year-old man, lame from birth, was healed by Peter and John early in their ministry. Peter restored Dorcas to the widows of the community by raising her from the dead. Eutychus, a young man who fell asleep sitting on the windowsill while listening to Paul's sermon and died when he fell to the ground, was resurrected to hear more, and perhaps to fall asleep again. People brought their sick into the street and laid them on beds and couches so that at least the shadow of Peter passing by might overshadow them. They brought the sick from rural areas into the city of Jerusalem, and everyone, including the demon-possessed, was healed (Acts 5:15, 16). The apostle James wrote that when a church member became sick, the family should call the elders to pray over him and to anoint him with oil. "And the prayer of faith shall save the sick, and the Lord shall raise him up; and if he have committed sins, they shall be forgiven him."

The Old Testament was equally assuring that God supported good health. Naaman the leper was healed by washing in the Jordan River seven times. The Shunamite's son was restored to life by Elisha. What better promise could we want than the words of the psalmist: "Bless the Lord, O my soul, and forget not all his benefits: who forgiveth all thine iniquities; who healeth all thy diseases" (103:2, 3).

As we read, there was born in us a hope, a trust in God,

that what he had done in the past, he was also able to do today. Friends encouraged us, sometimes hesitatingly, sometimes with bold assurance, to pray for healing. Surely God's will was health for Walter, since he is the great Physician and Walter was his child.

We were human, doubting as we believed. A new growth was constricting the large intestine, but in view of his past medical history, the doctors were reluctant to operate again. Without surgery the future remained uncertain. Each new symptom of ill health, regardless of how small it was, caused dark clouds of fear to descend. Yet we seemed to have no alternative but to move ahead with our former plans to continue Walter's education, and after that to accept the editorial position already offered him. I sometimes marvel now that we had the courage to make the long move to a new country and a new community and a new job; yet if we always knew the outcome of our decisions, wouldn't most of us sit paralyzed with fear and do nothing? Those who have experienced the push of the Spirit despite tremendous difficulties and even criticism will understand how we felt.

After six or seven weeks in Hillsboro, when the illness which had been in remission for some weeks revealed itself again, Walter felt led to ask the deacons of the church to anoint him with oil and to pray over him. It was no desperate last-ditch stand. It was simply obedience to the command of the Word of God. It was something we probably should have done earlier.

The men came. I don't remember their names because they were mostly strangers to me. I remember only that they seemed uncomfortable. Awkward. Trying to have faith for us. Hoping for a miracle for this young husband

and father, but not sure of themselves. I remember very little of my own feelings, except that I had become part of a scene being painted on a canvas no longer of my own choosing. Too much had happened in too short a time to grasp the significance of it all.

The older girls, who sensed the drama being played around them, reacted in their own ways. Joanna wrote later: "One evening, while we were eating supper, I looked at Daddy's face and I saw a skeleton there. I felt as if his spirit was beginning to leave his body and that he was now primarily decaying flesh. I felt unalterable sense of loss, and that evening I took a walk along the railroad tracks, grieving.

Thus, when the folks from the church came over to 'rebuke the devil' I felt that I was one up on them—they were deluded if they thought that they had any kind of power to change the immutable. Daddy was already partly gone from us and the process of transmission from this earth to the next life could not be reversed. I knew this, I felt this, I was utterly assured of this fact. I suppose my subsequent stoicism stemmed from it. I guess I figured, subconsciously, that there was no sense protesting what could not be changed anyway. I remember that I felt that those unholy men were performing some sort of desecration in the living room, with the body of my father the subject of their ritual. I felt a sense of shame that such a thing should happen. The whole thing seemed alien. I sensed very little of the religious nature of the ritual—it seemed more like magic to me than an attempt by spiritual men to use their faith as a weapon against evil."

Perhaps others felt the same way that evening.

For several days thereafter Walter felt considerably better. We were glad and thankful for each "better day." But then the pains and discomfort returned, and one evening I took Walter to the small local hospital, where he died approximately ten days later. In a sense, I think I was glad he could finally die and be released from this world's pain and uncertainty. His lot was considerably easier than mine.

For weeks I didn't dare face the question of why God hadn't healed Walter. I boxed the experience off in my mind, resigned to my new role as a "widow woman" and especially a poor widow with four small children. I was too busy picking up the tangled and broken strands of life to think much about the matter. Death had taken place. It was irrevocable. I could do nothing about restoring Walter to life. Why agonize over questions without answers?

As life became more tranquil, at times I was plagued by the unanswered question of why God had not healed. Why was I a widow and my children orphans? It didn't seem right that we should be denied the privilege of living with complete relationships as a family. Those who had encouraged us to pray for healing now remained silent and never discussed it with me. Had their faith evaporated so soon? Hadn't they been convinced of the rightness of their actions? Had we all been the deluded victims of fanaticism? Had our faith been in vain? Had they done what they did to humor us, like a parent with a whining child?

I felt it best to wait until God himself gave me an answer or at least peace of mind. Each day I tried to live in commitment to him, thankful that he was supplying our basic needs as a family adjusting to a new community.

Several years later, the community was thrown into unexpected turmoil when a wave of the charismatic movement hit a small segment of the church congregation. A young husband, the father of two small boys, decided to quit taking insulin for his diabetic condition because he believed that God had healed him. Two days later he died. Questions about faith healing saturated the thinking of our little community, composed of a strongly church-oriented and tradition-minded people. Faith healing was discussed, argued, pushed aside, supported, condemned. A man had died. Other people were tempted to make the same kind of foolish error. I knew then I had to dig up the old questions and put them properly to rest.

Why doesn't God heal when he's given the chance? The answers have come in very small bits and pieces. The faith that God would heal had taken us through a long, difficult time of illness. We had committed ourselves to God, knowing he was able, yet at no time demanding healing of him. That faith had kept hope alive in our hearts, without which life would have been nearly impossible. Life without any hope, even when faced by lingering illness, becomes a vast desert of despair.

When God doesn't answer prayer, including prayer for healing, some people suggest that the request was unwise. Had we asked and received no answer because we asked for the wrong motives, to spend what we would receive on our own pleasures (James 4:3)? The desire to live, to continue in the marriage relationship as a father and husband, to serve God with one's gifts, didn't seem like lustful desires to me. I discounted that argument at once.

One widow told me she had been accosted by a church member who felt certain that her husband had died because of the waywardness of their son. She was told that the Spirit had given this insight to bring the young man to his knees. My friend felt devastated to think of God working in such vengeful ways. Yet without doubt many people secretly blame themselves or are blamed by others for the death of a loved one, believing that someone's sins have kept God from answering prayer.

Other people may assume that sin in the life of the sick person has kept God from answering prayer. The apostle James wrote, "Confess your faults one to another, and pray one for another, that ye may be healed. The effectual fervent prayer of a righteous man availeth much" (5:16). Known sin should be confessed, but one cannot judge the spiritual life of a sick person by his sickness. Why do people think of illness as originating in sin? Clearly, the Old Testament includes stories connecting the two. Miriam's leprosy was believed to be punishment for her rebellious action against Moses. David's sin was punished by the death of the baby born of his adulterous union with Bathsheba. In the New Testament, however, Jesus answered his disciples' questions about the man blind from his birth, "Neither has this man sinned, nor his parents" (John 9:3). Though sin may be the reason God cannot answer prayer at times, it is presumptuous to come to this conclusion in any particular situation. Judgment is also cruel when sickness becomes a permanent member of a family, one who abides over all decisions, rules all activities, and determines most attitudes in the family.

"You didn't pray hard enough" or "You didn't have enough faith to be healed" is another answer sometimes given. When is faith big enough for healing? When is it like a mountain? When is it like a mustard seed? When do we know we have packed enough faith into the battered tin cup we hold out timidly to God, like a beggar on the street?

"We who are ill are often told that our illness is due to our lack of faith for healing," writes Martha Snell Nicholson in her biography, *Servant on a Sickbed*. "This seems me a cruel thing. Surely it is hard enough to be ill without being told that there is something wrong in one's spiritual life."

Does faith have to be big? Or should it be faith in a Big Person? Most Christians don't find it difficult to believe that God, who created the universe and set it in motion, also has power to prolong life by healing sickness. To believe that God is able is perhaps the least obstacle to healing. To believe in God is to believe in his omnipotence. God cannot be God without being all-powerful. So the problem is usually not whether God can heal, but whether he will heal this person who has this particular illness at this point in time. And sometimes because we desire it so much, we are certain that God will heal. To differentiate between faith and presumption is sometimes difficult. We may mistake our own zeal or earnestness for the faith needed for healing.

I came to see that people believe they can manufacture faith out of emotion like a miller making flour out of wheat. If you have the one ingredient, you can produce the other on demand. The kind of faith needed for healing, contrary to what is sometimes taught, is not something we appropriate if we feel like it, like a coat we put on to go out into a storm. No friend, loved one, minister or other spiritual leader can promise healing, as much as he would like to. It is not his to decide that healing is the most wonderful thing that could happen and would glorify God to the greatest degree. If he promises healing, he takes on the role of God. He challenges God.

Throwing away crutches, glasses, trusses, braces, or medicine on the assumption that God will heal is presumption, not faith. Faith ultimately leaves the matter of healing to God. It is a complete yieldedness, a relaxed attitude toward God, not a tenseness or a demanding attitude, daring God not to heal. The prayer of faith is the one that says, "Thy will be done," knowing that every promise of the Bible, even one like "The prayer of faith shall save the sick," is conditioned by the sovereignty of God.

Some leaders in the healing movement suggest that to pray "Thy will be done" is an escape clause, i.e., an attempt to play it safe and have a "way out" if God doesn't heal. "We don't protect our reputations by a pious half-hearted, 'Heal this person, God, if it be thy will,' " said Dr. Alfred Price of St. Stephen's Episcopal Church in Philadelphia in an interview about his ministry of healing. "Christ has said, 'I will heal your afflictions.' We believe him literally. And although we admit to our own lack of complete understanding of how to lay hold of his healing power under all circumstances, we feel definitely that, based on what Christ has told us in the New Testament, we are directed to proceed along the lines of total healing." But isn't total abandonment to God more desirable than trying to control the situation? Remember that when Jesus prayed in the garden of Gethsemane before his betrayal, he added the phrase, "nevertheless not as I will, but as thou wilt" (Matthew 26:39).

Well-meaning Christians have occasionally commented that widowhood was God's will for me, meaning that death was what God had intended for Walter. I find it hard to accept that God planned the illness, step by step, so that I would have the challenging opportunity to bring up the children alone. I cannot grasp that he, who sees the sparrow fall, deliberately wanted Walter's life snuffed out, yet this is what the statement, "This is God's will for you," actually means. Jesus never said to the sick, "This is God's will for your life." He was filled with compassion.

Some well-meaning friends tried to explain away the hurt by saying, "You asked God to raise our brother from his sick bed, so he raised him higher." A poor pun. Not much else.

Here's another: "If God didn't heal in this lifetime, he will heal Walter in the next." Not much comfort.

Sometimes intended comfort for not having been healed is couched in words like "Just wait a few years and you'll understand why Walter wasn't healed." At a time when one feels half-shredded by a giant sausage machine, such words offer little solace.

Buried beneath the problem of healing is the bigger problem of our desire to manipulate God. Some Christians aren't concerned with how God works in their lives; they simply want him to perform—any time, any manner. "Just get with it, Lord." Like pagans, they desperately want "magic" performed for their sake. They're willing to learn the right chants, the right combination of events, the right formula, to persuade God to change his laws to meet their needs.

Few people pass through life without wishing, at one time or another, consciously or unconsciously, that they could invoke some magic power to come to their aid. At no time is this more true than during a terminal illness. Only then it is never referred to as magic.

Years ago a minister's wife described an experience to a group of young women, of which I was a member. Funds had been exhausted, with no money in sight. The supply of groceries was low and the butter, in particular, had been completely used up. As she prepared supper for herself and her husband, she stood over the table with her open Bible held over the empty butter dish and breathed a prayer to God to send them some butter. She closed her eyes hoping that somehow God would provide. But he didn't, and the butter dish remained empty for that meal and for many thereafter.

I was then a young Christian, trying to glean from her talk the true essence of faith. I never suspected that a time would come when I too would be tempted to wave God's Word in his face and gently but firmly demand results. Yet the Word of God as a book or as individual verses is no magic key that opens heaven's storehouse when we brandish them before God.

When a loved one lies seriously ill, when a difficult decision must be made, when a son or daughter hasn't caught on to what life is all about and keeps messing it up, what is the solution?

If only we knew a few magic words. Presto! Life would be the way we want it. And if straight magic doesn't work, maybe God could be persuaded to perform every day the way he did for Gideon. All we'd have to do is put out the fleece each evening with the note to the milkman.

As a child, I shared with other youngsters an uneasy, if superficial, belief in superstition, ghosts, and magic. By avoiding black cats, the number thirteen, beginning a journey on Friday, we hoped that happiness would be our lot. Many carry that approach over into adulthood, never giving it open acceptance, but adopting little rituals or slogans to keep life safe and secure.

The late A. W. Tozer pointed out that Moses and the prophets of Israel aimed some of their most vigorous attacks against the Israelites' tendency to believe in superstition. He added that superstition is still one of the most serious threats to Christianity today. Without intending to, a person may slip into a pattern of belief that attributes spiritual power or value to material objects, or to the recitation of certain words, to carrying specific objects, to undertaking ritual actions, all in the hope that a higher power can be persuaded to act on one's behalf.

For example, Tozer continued, God had commanded the Jews to wear upon their persons selected passages of Scripture to remind them of their responsibility to obey the Word and to love the Lord above all. By the time of Christ, this practice had degenerated into pure superstition. The phylacteries in which the Scriptures were carried had taken on magical qualities and were considered a source of power in themselves.

The Protestant church has few religious objects to which its members might assign supernatural powers, yet we aren't free from superstition. Because we evangelicals place high value on the Bible as the Word of God, we are in danger of making the Scriptures a book of magic and the Christian life very mechanical and artificial.

I once knew a very sincere Christian woman who regarded the Bible as her personal magic guidebook, although she would have been horrified to have me say that about her. If she didn't know which direction the cows had headed at milking time, she opened the Bible at random, stuck her forefinger on a verse, and looked for wisdom about the ways of cows in that Scripture.

Some evangelicals seem to believe that Scripture verses attached to any kind of an object, however trivial, give the object greater value. A letter opener, a pencil, or ruler seems to become more worthwhile as a gift if it has "The Lord is my shepherd" parading down the side or back.

During Walter's illness, I became aware of the pressure of some radio and television ministers to persuade Christians to write for various semireligious objects, a mustard seed encased in plastic to be worn as a bracelet charm or an illuminated cross to hang in a sick person's bedroom to make faith more meaningful. Many carry their Bibles to the hospital, not to read them, but to have them there. I don't discount the comfort of having the Word near by, but I wonder about those who carry it around but never read it.

The Christian life is a meaningful relationship between a personal God and the individual who chooses to follow him, based on trust. It is an intelligent relationship. Christians should deliberately move away from a mechanical approach to Scripture. We need to allow the Spirit to use the meaning of the whole Bible to strengthen us to face our problems and to carry on. To use Scripture like some magic chant or potion is an attempt to manipulate God and constitutues a return to paganism.

Also related to the matter of healing is our tendency to draw the conclusion that God is defeated in death or in prolonged illness. Christians may believe that sickness is the worst evil and death a betrayal by God despite the ringing words of Scripture assuring us that death can be a victory for the believer. The Great American Dream has insidiously affected our thinking about spiritual health. Physical health, glowing health, is equated with spiritual success. A healthy Christian is one upon whom God's blessing rests. The person struggling with arthritis, ulcers, cancer, hardening of the arteries, and usually at the same time, financial problems, doesn't fit the pattern of the overcoming Christian.

Health equals holiness. A person has to be healthy to be considered really alive. This discovery shocked me. I had discovered a new oppressed minority. American ethics spells out clearly that personal success is rated by an individual's ability to climb economic and social ladders. Within the church, a person struggling with ill health is flawed somewhere, and therefore his contribution to the community of the saints isn't worth quite as much as that of the well person.

In her novel, *No Graven Image*, Elisabeth Elliot includes an incident about a young missionary who prays for the healing of a convert in an Indian tribe. She is convinced that his healing will be the determining factor in turning the whole tribe to God. The continuation of God's work seems to depend on this miracle. Yet the man dies.

Is God defeated when a man for whom his friends have prayed dies? Such experiences are not often heralded in church periodicals. After my article "When

God Does Not Heal" was published in a number of religious journals, I received many letters from readers thanking me for what I had written. God can make all things work together for good, including the experience of non-healing.

I will always be grateful to a kindly old minister for whom I did some copy editing, who was wise in the ways of God and man. As we talked about the vicissitudes of life one day, he said to me: "The miracle greater than healing is the faith in those left behind to continue life with courage." In a few years he suffered a stroke and was unable to walk or talk for the remaining years of life.

Our greatest need in sickness or in health is a living bond with God. If healing takes place, how tempted some people might be to trust, not in God, but in the experience of healing. Every experience of non-healing can be a testimony of grace and victory. Those who loved and prayed and hoped and waited and yet found death can react to the experience with faith or with bitterness. They can meet God in the experience or reject him. They need not claw at the empty space or resort to verbal juggling, talking about death only in euphemisms. God is not defeated because someone dies; death is not the final answer. The disciples saw the Cross of Calvary as the end of Christ's ministry. Satan had conquered. They returned to fishing, their occupation before Christ called them into his service. Yet on the resurrection day, the Cross became the beginning of life for all who believed.

I believe that God does heal the sick today. He is concerned about our arteries and acne, cancers and cankers. He uses many vehicles to heal—the surgeon's knife, medicines, psychiatric treatment, as well as what appear to be miracles. Any of these processes may set healing forces in motion. When we speak of faith healing, we are usually referring to the working of natural laws beyond human understanding and to the release of energies belonging to the divine or supernatural.

To believe that God is able to heal is not sufficient. Healing faith is not brought into existence by earnestness or presumption, like making an *A* with God because we have been good or done our homework well. We can't force ourselves by sheer willpower or intellectual strength or scriptural knowledge to achieve healing. It isn't something appropriated in desperation. Boldly asserting words of faith doesn't bring about healing any more than being sure one will win a sweepstakes. It's presumptuous to stop medical treatment and to insist that God will heal, asserting that we have the correct formula for God's working. The Scriptures yield no pattern, no categories, no sets of laws.

The prayer of faith that heals is a gift of God, according to the apostle Paul (1 Corinthians 12:9), a gift we cannot demand from God, and most certainly not a gift that is evoked by learning magic codes. As some have the gift of teaching or prophesying or leading, so some receive the gift of healing. And after it has been received, it must be nurtured.

We cannot assume that God will always heal. Sometimes he has other purposes in mind. If healing always took place, our churches would have the biggest business of the century going. Death would be obliterated, and hospitals bankrupt for lack of patients. Even Lazarus, beloved of Jesus, eventually had to die. Paul wasn't healed by the ministry of his physician friend, Luke, or by divine intervention. He had to live with his thorn in the flesh. Knowing that everyone must die at some time nevertheless shouldn't discourage anyone from praying or from seeking help from the medical profession. All knowledge is from God, including medical knowledge, and should be thankfully received. Prayer for healing should be part of the joint ministry of the medical profession, friends, ministers, and deacons. Too often it's a last resort.

Healing faith demands total commitment to God and to his will, acknowledgement that God can work his purposes through a sick person or a well one. He can make even the wrath of man to praise him. Such a commitment gives a person strength to face the difficulties of life and move forward, even though one is tempted to say with Mary, "Lord, if you had been here, my brother had not died."

Dr. Mary Verghese was injured in a car accident shortly before she was to graduate from medical school. She was left paralyzed from the waist down. In the biography, *Take My Hands*, Dorothy Clarke Wilson describes how Mary faced the prospect of her medical career being wiped out and of living a painful, empty, useless life. Job had affirmed, "Though he slay me, yet will I trust in him" (13:15). Mary Verghese's prayer was "Though he slay me *not*, yet will I trust him." Though she never regained use of her lower limbs, she returned to her profession as a surgeon on the hands of lepers in India, work she could perform sitting down. She dedicated to God all she had to give—her hands.

W. L. Carrington writes in *Psychology, Religion and Human Need*, "Only a faith which is willing to accept any or no healing can free the body and mind from emotional conflict with its constant dissipation of energy, and so liberate in its fullness the healing power of the spirit of God. That surely is what faith meant to Jesus, and it must mean that to those who are made whole." When the picture of life is completed, we will see the whole. If we have trusted in God rather than in faith or in an experience, we may find that there was purpose for what happened.

Years before his own death, Walter had commented on the death of a favorite Bible teacher and minister, Dr. A. H. Unruh. Walter wrote about life under the sun as being but a fragment: "It never attains perfection, fulfillment, full attainment. Is there a completeness about infancy, childhood, youth, man, the aged? Does life flower, come to a perfect cycle, or does it break off? Why should Dr. Unruh with his wisdom and experience now break off? He is only ready to begin."

The answers to such questions are in the mind of God.

The absurdities, the complexities of life can be answered only with continued faith that God will put the fragments together in time. We must continue to believe he is Lord even when we cannot understand. We must always keep him in the picture. If, during a difficult experience, because things don't turn out the way we desire, we shut him out, then evil is the last word. If we keep God in, the last word will be good and his truth the victor.

CHAPTER ELEVEN
When You Suffer

A measure of faith is whether you can look at life's darkness and yet believe in the light. —Anonymous

"Put your light on, Mommie, so I can come to you," called our four-year-old from his bedroom in the middle of the night. The moment my fumbling fingers found the switch, he was at my side to tell me his little need, which had seemed so big when all was darkness. When he found himself alone at night he needed a light to go to Mother.

A child of God may also grope in spiritual night. Circumstances, daily needs, and problems shroud him with a heavy blanket of darkness. His spirit cries to God to send light so that it may know where to find him.

Joseph lay in a musty cell in Pharaoh's prison and knew the darkness of what it means to be forgotten and in disrepute. Job experienced the darkness of physical pain, misunderstanding, and criticism of friends. His wife of many years hurled crushing words at him, "Job, you have sinned. Why try to hang onto your integrity? Curse God and die."

A mother who has waited and prayed for years for her son to change the direction of his life senses an overshadowing of her spirit as she watches him grow more determined to give his life to empty goals rather than to God.

Who can measure the dark loneliness when a husband or wife, a child or parent is taken by death, or when one daily watches a loved one grow weaker through physical suffering?

A woman I knew had wanted to be a teacher, but circumstances, including the care of her sick mother, forced her to work in a factory. Many years went by. When her mother died, she was suddenly free, but then she was too old to begin teaching. Her cry came from her soul's darkness, "Why did this have to be my way? Why couldn't I fulfill my lifelong ambition?" Has God an answer?

We joke about the inevitability of death and taxes as being the common denominator of man. We cannot escape either. But when death draws a step closer and takes someone dear, we must choose more carefully our attitude to death and dying and suffering.

F. B. Meyer tells a beautiful old legend of a Hindu woman whose only child died. Distraught, she came to Buddha and pled with him to restore life to her boy. His reply, kindly given, was to ask her to bring him a handful of rice from a home which death had never entered. Then he would grant her request.

She began her search at once and went from dwelling to dwelling, bearing her pathetic burden. At each place, she asked the question, "Are you all around the hearth —father, mother, children—none missing?" Invariably all sadly shook their heads. As she passed from house to house, her own grief subsided before the specter of sorrow all about her. She accepted the death of her child, buried it, and took up the duties of the living.

As Christians we are confident that death brings the believer into the presence of the Lord. We have faith to believe that death in Christ is a glorious victory. The problem, however, of how to face the loss of a loved one seems harder to solve. How can life without that person also be victory in Christ?

Two ways are open to the person who suffers. Anyone who has faced the death of a close member of the family knows about them. There is the way of rebellion and bitterness, and the way of acceptance and submission. One way leads to greater darkness; the other to light.

Of course, these ways don't appear as clearly marked paths to the person who is suffering. At first, every day may seem to be a dreary wasteland with aching loneliness hanging over the spirit. Aimlessness may invade every aspect of life, so that the person in grief feels he doesn't know how to act. Unless the Spirit of God is present to guide, he may move blindly in the direction of rebellion.

One of the difficult matters to accept is what appears to be the gross unfairness of a situation created by death, illness, or other circumstance. Why should homes be robbed of parents, parents never see their children grow to manhood and womanhood, young children never know the love of grandparents, the needy denied the loving care of a Dorcas? Americans have been led to believe that life owes each person a square deal: long life together, good health, fine children, vacations abroad, and a paid-up home. When this pattern is disrupted, the person caught in the middle is tempted to demand justice. "Life isn't fair. Why must I carry this burden while others go free?" The temptation is greater when one has to enter the crucible of suffering time and time again.

Shortly after Walter's death, my second daughter, Susan, became ill with a stomachache one morning during vacation Bible school. The next day she felt better, so back she went to classes, games, Kool-Aid, and cookies. Two weeks later, one Monday morning after I'd gone to work, Christine phoned me to say that Susan was very sick. Would I come home? Late that evening the doctor performed an emergency operation to drain the pus from a ruptured appendix, which had probably burst two weeks earlier. Twice in one family! I couldn't believe it.

But Susan lived—to escape death a second time that summer on a vacation trip to Glacier National Park. With some friends we stopped at a mountain stream to watch the water careening down the gully. The moment the cars stopped, all the children rushed out of the cars to the banks of the little river. Susan slipped on the moss, still wet with early dew, fell into the water, and was immediately carried downstream by the force of the current. I stood at the bank horrified, not knowing what to do. An older nephew ran alongside the stream and pulled her out at a lower spot. That summer a second surgery was performed to remove the stub of the appendix.

Another summer I had major surgery. Another summer my oldest child, who had never been able fully to accept her father's death, had an emotional breakdown and required psychiatric treatment. Enough is enough, I thought. At some point this summer-sickness has to stop.

One wintry day in February after a violent Kansas storm, my third child complained of pains in her arms and legs. We had all been shoveling snow to clear the driveway, so I dismissed her pains lightly. My arms and back ached too. Her pains continued, and the doctor at first diagnosed her illness as rheumatoid arthritis. I felt as if someone had doused me with pails of ice water. Chris, the gentle and quiet one, the one who seemed least able to cope with a long-term difficult disease. My heart ached as if someone had driven a spike into it. As months wore on, her condition became no better. In fact, when it became acute, necessitating a lengthy stay in the hospital, we looked for other medical help. This time the diagnosis, later confirmed by the National Institutes of Health at Bethesda, Maryland, was systemic lupus erythematosus, a chronic disease that can affect almost any organ. That spike in my heart was surely and deftly being twisted to cause the utmost pain.

I can think of no other time when I felt so discouraged and exhausted. I was tired of sickness, tired of raising children by myself, tired of going to school (I had been working on a master's degree in English at a nearby university), tired of housekeeping by twilight, tired of speaking at women's groups, tired of writing. Life just wasn't worth it any more. I was ready to ditch everything except maybe the opportunity to come before God with my list of complaints. Lord, you promised to be a father to the widows and fatherless. You promised to be with those who kept faith in you. Now, where are you and all your promises?

When we suffer, it's easy to slip into the temptation to blame it all on God. He is the only all-powerful personality we recognize. Satan is not usually a clear concept to us, nor are we constantly aware that we are in a fight against evil and the forces of evil. Because God is the person in control, we blame him for what has happened.

When we put our trust in God but are laid flat by circumstances, how can we reconcile this with the love, mercy, and justice of God? It's less difficult to fit a martyred missionary into our faith than to watch a child suffer with leukemia. The death of Christ on the cross makes sense, but not the anguish of an older Christian who, after many years of service, is losing his reasoning powers because of hardening of the arteries.

It isn't unusual for someone to come into a home where a Christian is suffering and to say, "This is the will of God." Or, if a patient dies, to say at the time of the death, "This was the will of God," but then later mention to friends, "If better medical help had been available, John might have lived." If it was the will of God to die, it can't also be the will of God to live. Using the phrase "the will of God" seems to be a euphemism for saying, "God is responsible for this."

When three children were killed in a schoolhouse collapse, their father screamed curses against God because of their death. He later found that a corrupt local government, to save money, had allowed shoddy material to be used for the building.

A young boy was killed while playing in a garage in which a loaded shotgun was hanging. His parents wrote an obituary which appeared in a church paper. "We know this was God's way of taking our son to him."

A young child died in a highway accident. The mother was told: "This is God's will for you. God took your child. He wanted her more than you do." A young man died of leukemia. His parents were told: "God knew to whom he could give this experience. He knew you could take it." Behind all these accounts is the concept of a God who is demanding, vengeful, and who willingly sends calamity and hardship to his children.

It is important to keep clear the character of God. We all have some kind of theology or concept of God, and we live accordingly. Our relationship to God is based on our knowledge and understanding of him.

If we think of God as an ecclesiastical figure, we limit the life of faith and trust to the sphere of the local church. The church is God's realm. The human realm is on the outside where things are practical and sensible. For people with such a concept of God, the call of the church is a call to participate in its services and programs. The church then becomes a competitor with that outside world for time, money, and loyalty.

If we think of God as a God of nature, whom we meet in the beauty of the forest, the mountains, the flowers of the fields, and the sound of the sea, we may indulge in a kind of natural religion, assuming that a return to the great outdoors is a return to God.

Some people conceive of God as a kind grandpa sitting in a rocker in heaven, handing out goodies when the children come to visit him. Or else they may think of him as a sort of super-Batman who can do anything he wants to. He can rush in on his angel-powered Batmobile and help people out of any kind of pinch, or maybe even turn a pair of mice into a new Volkswagen.

Belief in a personal devil has receded in past decades. When faced with unexplainable problems, some people don't know what else to do but attribute to God everything evil and terrible in their lives: sickness, hardship, calamity caused by natural causes or personal carelessness. Thereby they turn God into a devil, the originator of evil.

The modern church needs a greater understanding of the nature of God. Without question we also need a clearer concept of the devil and how he operates in the twentieth century. We especially need to recognize that the Christian life is a warfare against evil, for which we need the total armor of God. Living in a society riddled with corruption and openly denying the existence of God, those who claim to be his disciples have to recognize that he is a loving God who also acts in judgment. Our great God who created the world and all its beauty hasn't stepped out of the universe and history to watch his handiwork unfold without him. He is a loving, powerful, omniscient God, still deeply involved in the world he created, even though wars, famines, illnesses, untimely deaths, floods, and tornados seem to indicate to some people that he has deserted his creation.

During my own times of discouragement and defeat, I became more clearly aware of both God and the devil. I discovered that Satan will use anything to defeat us, even below-the-belt punches. His tactics with widows are especially effective. F. B. Meyers has said, "All discouragement is of the devil." The devil knows that a discouraged or dissatisfied person, whether a lowly widow or a prominent preacher, is useless to the work of God's kingdom. Satan doesn't want us to connect our discontent over circumstances with him. He prefers to have us blame our troubles on God. The devil will try to keep a widow indifferent to the riches of a fuller spiritual life through sorrow or frustration or bitterness. If she is satisfied with superficial living, he isn't too concerned that she'll hunger to know what God can really mean to her life.

Nor is Satan anxious to change his image in our mind. Many people think of him as the red, horned individual with a long curling tail and a three-pronged fiery fork, whose environs are whorehouses, gambling tables, and hit joints. As long as we think the devil's main beat isn't where we are, he needn't fear being recognized when he moves into the pleasant residential sections of town, tempting men and women to discouragement and dissatisfaction. Some widows, disgruntled with their circumstances, find a scapegoat in the "widow syndrome": "After all, I'm only a widow. What else do you expect of one so battered by life?"

The story is told that one day Satan appeared before Martin Luther to tempt him. Luther recognized his enemy, snatched an inkwell from his desk, and hurled it at his tempter. The devil fled. Luther may have sent him flying, but he didn't kill him. Like Luther, we need to chase him from our private domain with any weapon we have. Christ conquered Satan by his death and resurrection. We need to let every dissatisfaction, disappointment, or frustration be an opportunity for God's grace to triumph. In faith, we need to throw whatever we can at Satan, for he's a defeated enemy. One day I threw my typewriter at him, so to speak. I began to write again. My healing began when I recognized that my enemy wasn't God, but Satan.

Much of the suffering we experience in life is the result of human willfulness and sin. Yet we attribute to God the limitations set upon our lives by all suffering and sorrow. I have always done a lot of reading, especially in times of perplexity. I wish I could give credit to all the books which together have formed my *Weltanschauung*, but I can't. I remember one writer who pointed out that we may have gotten the impression that God wills evil because of the excellent way Christian saints have handled suffering. They have produced such remarkable beauty out of ashes that we credit God with the evil that made possible so much good. Such thinking brings God in at the wrong point. He should be credited with the grace and power that redeemed the evil and produced good in the lives of his children. He should be credited with what they did within their limitations, by following his direction.

I recommend that anyone struggling with basic questions of belief and problems of life should turn to some of the great classical writers of the church. Their books aren't cluttered with cultural concepts, nor disdainful of society, nor occupied with narrow religious doctrine. Such writings help us to be realistic about faith and self and the world. What is more, a spirit of joy permeates them. In these old writings I found many clues to the mystery of suffering.

It was clear to me that God hadn't willed Walter's death or the illness of the other children. But I still had to figure out how to handle the problem of suffering in relation to God. I read Hannah Whitall Smith's books and those by Watchman Nee, Henry Scougal, Leslie Weatherhead, and others. They helped me establish a theological base for my thinking.

As I studied the Old Testament, I saw that the saints of those days attributed everything in their lives to God, both good and bad. Years after his slave experience and prison experience, Joseph could say to his brothers, "Now therefore be not grieved, nor angry with yourselves that you sold me hither: for God did send me before you to preserve life" (Genesis 45:5). I stumbled over this passage, which seemed to make God the originator of evil in the hearts of the brothers.

"Is God in everything?" asks Hannah Smith. How can a Christian accept this truth when nearly everything in life comes to us through human instrumentality and most of our problems are the result of somebody's failure, ignorance, carelessness, or sin? We know that God can't be the author of these things, yet unless he is the agent in the matter, how can we say to him about it, "Thy will be done"?

She was asking my question.

Our answer depends on our attitude. We need to see God in everything and to receive all of life from his hands, with no intervention of "second causes" (brothers who sell us into slavery, Babylonians who force us into exile, the sin of mankind that brings sickness into the world, children who disobey, neighbors who pry). God has permitted the circumstances, good or bad. He didn't cause or will them, but he permits them. He is the sovereign God. The Jews had to accept seventy years' exile as from God, when actually the Babylonians were responsible. They could have discounted God entirely, but in

Mrs. Smith's words, "There are no second causes."

Have we warrant from Scripture to accept everything from the hands of God without regard for these second causes, human or otherwise (*i.e.*, evil forces)? Take the story of Joseph as an example. Sin was responsible for his brothers' action; and therefore what they did couldn't be said to be the will of God. Yet by the time it worked itself out in Joseph's life, he could see how God had used their sin for his good and theirs.

The New Testament supports such a view of life. The apostle Paul wrote to the Romans, "We know that all things work together for good to them that love God, to them who are the called according to his purpose" (8:28). The verse I had focused on that winter day in Ontario when Walter first became sick leaned in the same direction: "In every thing give thanks: for this is the will of God in Christ Jesus concerning you." That "everything" meant good things and bad.

I saw this principle at work in day-to-day experiences. One woman, who called frequently in our home, would often leave me in tears with her carefully worded statements that seemed to point out my every inadequacy as a mother, housekeeper, church worker, and child of God. How could I ever be thankful for her? It gradually became clear that if I received evil as from humankind, I entered into conflict with her, resulting in hard feelings. If I could receive that woman's interference in my life as something that God had allowed, I was free from conflict with her. I was responsible only to God. What glorious freedom and independence! Talking to a psychologist later on, I found out that psychology supports such an attitude. If we allow ourselves to be upset by another person, then that person controls our attitudes and possibly our actions. Freedom comes when we can disengage ourselves from conflict and bondage to people.

"So now it was not you that sent me hither, but God," said Joseph to his brothers, although he knew what had actually happened. "Thus faith, in the last analysis," writes Erick Sauer in *The Arena of Faith,* "accepts nothing from the hands of men; faith accepts all things from the hands of a great, loving, almighty, ruling God, including all the difficulties, losses, injustices . . . For this reason the Scriptures never speak of a mere 'permissive' will of God. His attitude is not passive in the happenings of this world, but definitely active. He is not beside the events, but in them."

Anxiety and pain are part of life, yet suffering remains a mystery, part of which is the recognition that pain has a deep purpose in the community of the children of God. Dr. Paul Brand, working with lepers in India, at one point in his career feared he had contracted the disease from his patients. One day he discovered that, like a leper, he had no feeling in the heel of his foot. Later, when he jabbed a pin into his ankle and experienced pain, the relief of that blessed pain was staggering. He thanked God for it.

As he continued to work with lepers, he discovered that the loss of their fingers and toes wasn't due to the disease, but because they could feel no pain. Rats might chew off the insensate extremities, or physical injury cause the loss of flesh. Without pain to warn them, they were unaware of what was happening to their fingers and toes. The pain we experience because of another's suffering tells us we belong together.

In an old story which took place during the Middle Ages, a rabbi told his disciples that he had learned the meaning of love that day by listening to two peasants in the village.

"What did they say?" asked one of his students.

"The first one asked his friend, 'Tell me, Ivan, do you love me?' 'Yes, I do,' said the second one. 'Do you know what gives me pain?' asked the first. 'Pray,' asked the second, 'how can I know what gives you pain?' The first one again replied, 'If you do not know what gives me pain, how can you love?' "

So the teacher said to his disciples, "Understand then, my sons, to love truly means to know what brings pain to your comrade."

Earlier I mentioned two approaches to suffering: bitterness or acceptance. The pathway of acceptance, the one that leads to God, looks for a way to turn heartache and limitation into beauty and freedom. Life thus becomes an adventure of faith. Both Hannah Smith and A. B. Simpson once again guided me through these truths. Mary's accusing words to Christ had been my words, "Lord, if thou hadst been here, my brother had not died." Christ could have been at the sisters' home, but he wasn't. Christ could have made the situation different, but he didn't. Instead, Christ met Mary's "if" with his "if." "Said I not unto thee, that, if thou wouldest believe, thou shouldest see the glory of God" (John 11:40). Simpson suggests that the person who is confronting God with an "if" should make a power out of that "if" for God. "Face the 'if' in your life and say, 'For this I have Jesus.' " For the suffering and hurt of widowhood, I have Christ.

Soon after I became a widow I realized that many attitudes toward widowhood are passed on lovingly from one widow to another. Lonely people talk to other lonely people about their loneliness. Self-pity thrives on sympathy. The first challenge before me was to get out of what some have called the widow's rut. I had to offer my suffering to God so that some good could come out of it. Widowhood can be a prison in which the individual welds the bars a little stronger each day by attitudes of bitterness for what has happened. Widowhood can also be what Hannah Smith called a chariot that will take us to high places. She directed my attention to the passage in Scripture in which Elijah's servant saw the armies of the enemy surrounding the city. He was frightened. But the prophet sat calm and unafraid in his house. The servant was intimidated because he could see only the outward and visible; the prophet could see the inward and invisible. So Elijah prayed to the Lord to open the servant's eyes and show him the horses and chariots of God waiting to take them to victory in battle. Widowhood—a prison or a chariot? Faith can make the difference.

Acknowledging God's hand in one's life isn't an attitude of blind fatalism. He can use even your painful circumstances to glorify himself. What has happened, has happened. You don't know why. You can't change the situation, but with faith you can accept it, knowing that a sovereign and loving God permitted it. Such acceptance brings the assurance that he is still in control after death has become part of the family. He has said, "I will never leave thee, nor forsake thee" (Hebrews 13:5). Our Father is the husbandman. It is no stranger or enemy who holds the pruning knife. "God is faithful, who will not suffer you to be tempted above that you are able" (1 Corinthians 10:13).

Norman Grubb in *Touching the Invisible* writes that adversity can be the doorway into God's most transcendent secret. The secret is that adversities and sufferings, which in their origin are the effects of sin and instruments of the devil, become redemptive in the grasp of faith. Instead of being something to be endured, they can through faith become an instrument of good. This is the meaning of the Cross: death is transformed into life.

Many years ago a friend told me a story of what she had learned through suffering. She had given birth to a baby in a small rural community hospital. After a long and difficult labor, the doctor had finally delivered the child with forceps, causing its head to be badly bruised. The severe trial of entrance into this world left the infant weak, and when on its back, its eyes fell backwards so that only the whites could be seen, giving it a vacant look.

Because the mother was also weak, her stay in the hospital was prolonged. Many visitors came to see her and her newborn infant. They would visit with her and then go next door to see another patient. Lowered voices floated back to her: "Her child is blind . . . an idiot . . . deaf . . . it has a waterhead." Overhearing these whispers, she prayed that the Lord might give her grace to care for such a baby. She wanted to be able to love him and present him to the children waiting at home as the dear little brother for whom they had longed.

In due time she took her baby home and still the visitors came—to see her but also to see the child. Her burden increased when her children came home from school in tears, telling how other youngsters had derided their baby brother. Her spirits sank lower each day.

Some of her friends even encouraged her to sue the doctor, but she felt that the Lord wanted her to bear this burden herself. Further, the doctor tried to convince her that in a matter of weeks the baby would be normal.

One day the minister came to see her. Inwardly she could hardly bring herself to show him her child, but prayerfully, she picked up the infant, and placing a pillow under its head so that its neck and head were firmly supported, brought it to him. In this position, the baby's eyes remained in normal position. The minister looked at the child and said, "Well, if it's no worse than this, then what the people are saying is all wrong."

As other visitors came, she did the same. Soon the rumors stopped. In about six weeks, the child was almost well. He grew up to be a healthy, well-developed young man of normal intelligence. But in those difficult first weeks, she experienced what many parents must suffer when they realize that their child isn't normal. She had learned love and understanding by choosing not to nurse dark, bitter thoughts. She had accepted sorrow with sweetness and grace. As always, a dignity, beauty, and glory separate the two attitudes.

In the years since Walter's death, I have learned many lessons. I have learned a lot about selfishness and something about love and forgiveness. I have learned I cannot demand release from suffering for myself or others. I have learned that I cannot decide for a child how she will handle suffering. (My daughter Chris has often been my source of comfort. She has often pointed me to the Source of strength, comfort, and wisdom.) I have learned I cannot force my children to choose the God I have chosen to believe in. I have learned I cannot determine the way they will go, nor do I want to. I have learned that suffering can draw together and bring about a warm relationship between two people; it can also estrange. I remember one funeral at which the new widow gave a glowing account of the events leading to her husband's death and her feelings of triumph. I have often wished I could shout from the housetop some of the words of complete victory and strength I hear other widows say.

I recognize humbly that I am human and that God is God, but that it is possible to go from strength to strength. Though one may pass through the valley of Baca, one can transform it into a life-giving well (Psalm 84:6, 7).

The father of a retarded child said, "Once I thought maybe this child was sent to us as a punishment for our past misdeeds or something. Then I realized that was wrong—that God is a God of love, not somebody thinking up fiendish ways to make people suffer. Now I realize that because of our little boy, who will never grow up, every member of our family is a better person. I'm a lot more unselfish and tolerant than I ever dreamed I would be. We had to devote our lives to helping him; otherwise, all those efforts would have been channeled into helping ourselves."

The late literacy missionary, Frank Laubach, described how he often pondered the question of suffering and what seemed like such a waste of human lives. One day he had been trying all afternoon to teach a native boy to read, but trying to train the boy's mind seemed to be like pouring water into a mosquito net. Why, he asked, must some people be blessed with so much intelligence that thoughts pour from them as easily as one pours coffee, and others are so stupid and dull. "O God, what is all this wreckage for?" The answer he received from God: "The wreckage is the birthpangs of love." Suffering can give birth to divine love and understanding. Out of the wreckage of the lives Dr. Laubach worked with, he learned a little more about how love is created.

On second thought, that is perhaps what I learned also.

CHAPTER TWELVE
Be My Comforter

Who knows at what point of discouragement the simplest act of love may reach a soul and turn it again to to the light?
—Anonymous

Our comfortable American way of life has little room for suffering, sorrow, or loneliness. We have a tendency to avoid people with such needs. Poverty of the human soul is never pleasant. Perhaps we shy away from some people because we recognize our inadequacy to meet their need. "I wouldn't know what to say" is our excuse for staying home. By avoiding the suffering of others, we weaken our love and understanding of real people; yet we find emotional outlets in the pseudosuffering of television, movies, and novels.

The ministry of comforting is needed as much today in our prosperous society as it was 2,000 years ago when Dorcas made garments for the poor to lessen their burden. What is needed in our land is not always clothes for people's bodies, but spiritual salve to soothe their spirits, words of healing for souls sick with the problems of life.

Suffering is real and widespread, despite the good acting with which many people cover up their inner turmoil. People suffering with fears, loneliness, or disappointment may live just over the back fence or down the street, and you may never know it. The family in which I grew up in northern Saskatchewan knew little illness. We went through the usual round of childhood diseases, one sudden appendectomy, and a few tonsillectomies which a doctor decreed when they were medically fashionable. Headaches were unknown. They were a luxury we weren't permitted to indulge in because Mother believed that headaches were only for adult neurotics. As a result I never swallowed an aspirin until I left home. I learned to know real sickness only after I had been married about twelve years.

Although my husband was the only family member physically sick, his illness became a burden the whole family had to share, from the youngest toddler up. We were often in need, without always being able to identify our need clearly to ourselves or to others. We just ached.

Many people helped during the long days of my husband's illness. They came with food and flowers, money and moral support. I am grateful. Others wanted to help but didn't know how. Still others stood back in actual fear of what was taking place in our lives.

Friends have frequently asked me how they can help a widow or other person in the process of grief. They want the right words to say to erase the grief or make life easier. Grief is a long process that cannot be hurried. There are helping words, but no formula words, and the same words will not always do for each situation. I have tried to accept kindly the glib statements such as, "Don't worry, everything will turn out all right." To a person grieving, words like that ring empty and shallow. At the moment, nothing is all right. "You will soon find some-one to take Walter's place," said another. I didn't want anyone to take his place. One visitor was determined to clarify how Walter's death was God's way of dealing with me and bringing me closer to him. She kept shoving her knife deeper into my wound, convinced she was helping me. My only wish was that she would leave and never come back.

Leave censure and judgment up to God. Strange as it may seem, when a family is thrust again and again into the crucible of suffering, one whisper certain to mingle with many others is "I wonder what they did to have God make them suffer so." When a well-loved minister sud-denly died under tragic circumstances, one deacon took it upon himself to question each family member closely to find the Achan in the camp. He didn't bring the dead man back to life, but he added bitterness to their sorrow. You can be sure that the family will already have agonized over the question of why. Pray for them, but leave judging to God. Don't try to make those involved blame themselves for what has happened.

Don't expect those in need to ask freely for help, even if you've told them, "Call on me if there's anything I can do." When a person feels battered by circumstances, it's hard to ask for help. It's an open admission of inadequa-cy. A strong temptation for the person in sorrow is to shut herself away from life and nurse her grief. Or she may build a wall of defense around herself, reluctant to get back into the stream of life fully for fear of being hurt again. If you want to help, decide on what you think will be suitable and do it. The assistance I found easiest to accept was in the form of concrete offers such as "I'll take care of the children for you on Friday evening" or "I'll pick up the ironing tomorrow." Such love-offers couldn't be turned down.

Though a family may have carried the burden of an invalid or a retarded child in the home for decades, to think they are used to it or that it has become a painless procedure is a fallacy.

A fisherman's wife in Britain was preparing eels for market. One by one she picked up the live eels from the tub before her and with the aid of a sharp knife, stripped the skins from the wriggling creatures. A bystander remonstrated that it must be a painful procedure for the eels.

"Oh, no," she responded. "Not at all, I've been doing this now for over twenty-five years, and I am sure they're used to it."

Few families with serious problems ever become callous. By the grace of God they learn to live with them, but comfort is needed as much the tenth year as it was at the beginning.

Remember that a convalescent, a patient, or person in grief gets tired of describing his or her condition to all inquirers. My daughter Chris decided that to avoid a dismal repeating of her state of health to each person who visited her in the hospital, she should have a placard around her neck describing her condition as of that date, or a daily tape recording she could switch on when someone asked, "How are you?"

If you wish to be a comforter try to understand the real human needs of people living under the dark cloud of illness or sorrow. Place yourself on the sick person's bed. You will find that he is very sensitive to the attitudes of those around him and to those who come to see him and those who don't. He is often ambivalent about his own feelings. For awhile, a shorter or longer time, he has had to set aside his goals and hopes for the future. He feels ashamed of his dependence upon others. He worries that he has become a burden of time, money, and energy to those he should be helping. His family will often feel both guilty and helpless at not being able to keep up the sick person's spirits. At times they have mixed feelings of love and hatred for the invalid. They may become impatient and irritated that recovery takes so long. They may feel embarrassed at the weak answers they must give to visitors about future plans and so forth.

Inwardly, if not out loud, both the sick person and his family will be asking such questions as: How long will this sickness last? Could it possibly be malignant? Might it even be fatal? How will we meet the expenses? How will this affect the children? Does God really care what is happening to us?

Families in which some member has been sick for a long time agree that family life virtually comes to a standstill as the illness runs its course. All energy, activity, and thought are directed to the one big need in the home, to get the sick person well. After the crisis—either healing or death—the structure of family activities must be rebuilt once again.

A small example of this took place one Christmas when my James, then six, woke up one morning looking like a well-fed pocket gopher. He had the mumps. Mentally I went to the calendar and crossed out all activities for the next week to ten days, activities we had all looked forward to for some time. We would enjoy no Christmas dinner with the family, no Christmas Eve program. There was nothing to do except stay at home.

When an illness is serious and lengthy, the enforced social starvation can embitter family members, resulting in hard feelings toward the sick person. Suffering is never isolated. It reaches its tentacles into the lives of everyone closely connected with the patient. What children in such a home feel keenly, but perhaps don't express, is that homes without illness have a dignity that the home with a sick person, particularly a chronically sick person, can never achieve.

Going visiting as a complete family is impossible, nor can such a family invite company for Sunday dinner if the mother is an invalid. Picnics are almost out of the question, because it's no fun if only half the family is present. Even a birthday party lacks punch if the frolicking and laughter must be limited.

Children from homes where sickness is present compare themselves with children of "well" homes. From such comparisons can be born resentments, impatience, and even hatred, unless a comforter directed by God can help meet some of their needs for social fellowship.

This need of social fellowship has always been our greatest need as a family and my greatest need personally. Incomplete family units somehow don't fit into society as easily as "whole" families. The community in which we found ourselves had a strong tradition of visiting, especially at noon on Sundays. As a new widow with my four children, I was invited out often that first winter. I appreciated getting to know many new people during that period, but mostly the older couples did the inviting, not families with children. My children sometimes dreaded their Sunday excursions into adult-land. I appreciated immensely the occasions when friends went shopping with me to acquaint me with stores in the vicinity, or when we could mix with families with children.

The eighty-two-year-old father of a friend had never once experienced a serious illness. When family members became ill, he "pshawed" the cards, visits, and flowers they received as unnecessary frills. In his ninth decade he was hospitalized for the first time. He came out of that hospital with new understanding of the needs of the sick.

Dorothea Waitzmann, who battled the handicap of cerebral palsy, mentions in her book *A Special Way of Victory* how people regarded her at times as less than a whole person, a sort of second-class individual with inferior mentality, incapable because of her illness of feeling what others felt. God will use you as a comforter if you accept sick people and those who struggle with a loved one's illness not as people who have dropped down the scale of values on the human ladder but as whole and worthwhile people in God's sight.

If you would be a comforter, have faith to believe that you can communicate spiritual strength to those with burdens. God says in his Word that this is possible. Believe that God will use you. "God comforts us in all our tribulation, that we may be able to comfort them which are in any trouble, by the comfort wherewith we ourselves are comforted of God" (2 Corinthians 1:4). Have faith that love will draw and reassure the one in need of the love of God.

But when you move in to help, distinguish between mere pity for suffering and true comfort which is encouragement and stimulation to the burdened person. Self-pity is sin, for when a person pities himself he indicates he doesn't believe that God is sufficient for his particular need. The pity of others heaped upon self-pity is also wrong. When Christ told Peter that he would have to go to Jerusalem, and suffer many things and be killed, Peter, out of pity for his Lord, blurted out, "Be it far from thee, Lord; this shall not be unto thee." Although Peter couldn't accept suffering for his Lord, Christ refused to accept Peter's words of sympathy.

The invitation of friends to indulge in self-pity is one of the most difficult battles a widow fights. "How are you?" friends ask. In their kindness they are looking for small signs of weakness and dependence so that they can show love, so that they can be useful. Although many people are genuinely kind and concerned, some are always ready with sympathy as a substitute for love: "It must be terribly hard living alone." "Don't you get lonely by yourself?" "Are you getting along all right?" "How do you manage to be both father and mother to your children?"

The answer to the last question is that I don't. I try only to be the children's mother. If I accept sympathy even slightly, I know that my day will go down in defeat. There is no room for self-pity in a single person's life, widowed or otherwise. The happiest women I know are those who have refused to surrender meekly and have held the doctrine that each person has a contribution to make to life, married or single.

True comfort won't send a burdened person deeper

into despair and self-pity, but will lift and encourage and help him to see a God who is able to meet their need.

I remember the time when I faced the birth of our first child and the unknown experience before me. A tiny, white-haired grandmother, her face lined by many years of hard work, sensed my fear. She gave me six words of advice. My younger friends told me what to expect at the hospital, how many diapers and nighties I would need, and all about formulas and night-feedings. This mother and grandmother many times said simply, "The Lord helps at such times."

With these words she built a bridge by which I could walk in faith into one of the deepest experiences of a woman's life. She was telling me that when a woman needs God, he is there to help. All ten of her own children had been born at home, miles away from the white sterility of a hospital. Perhaps she was thinking of the time one of her babies arrived in the dead of winter in the old frame homestead on the cold, snowswept prairies. Perhaps she was reminded of the time she held a limp, feverish little girl in her arms on a hot, dry August day to watch her breathe her last. Whatever had been her own experience, she was offering me faith, steadied by courage. I thank my mother-in-law for her words of comfort and strength.

When you visit the sick and the sorrowing, ask God to guide you to the exact words to say and to what you should do. Don't feel you have to prove your Christianity to the person in need. God doesn't require this of you. How often I've felt embarrassed for people who stumbled for spiritual clichés on encountering me and couldn't find them.

Experiences of deep grief and sorrow, especially when coupled with deep faith, are a temptation to pry into. Don't force friends to reveal their deep feelings unless they're willing. Let time open their lips.

There is really only one approach to the suffering of others, and that is that it is a gift of God to enrich your life. God has a redemptive purpose for you in any affliction that moves into your life through the hardships of others. Our modern way of living has pushed all association with suffering out of our homes. We are born and we die in a hospital, sometimes in cruelly impersonal surroundings. Birth, sickness, death, and sorrow are no longer intimately a part of life in the immediate family circle. As we have yielded up our sick, our dead, and our newborn to institutions, we have also given over to specialists the ministry of comforting. Anthropologist Margaret Mead states in *Women and Mass Society:* "The ancient occupation of bathing the dead is now in the hands of morticians, a male profession conducted for profit. Midwifery is now in the hands of male obstetricians, followed by male pediatricians. Visiting the widowed and the sorrowful is done largely by male insurance agents—again as part of the profit structure."

Behind the pleasant faces we see all about us are often hearts in turmoil. Only the touch of another hand and sound of a human voice can help their need. Until I went through the experience of death and numerous illnesses, I didn't realize what an awful thing it is to live alone with a fear. The pastor in Alan Paton's *Cry the Beloved Country,* fearful about what may have happened to his son, says, "Fear is a very long journey, sorrow is at least an arriving." Long? It is endless. Older people on the waning edge of life live in fear of the days they will be completely desolate, useless to themselves and others. Some single women envision immeasurable years with loneliness as their constant companion. Young mothers can sometimes be among the loneliest people. During the baby years they seem to lose touch with the world swiftly passing by, while they're coping with bottles, diapers, and baby's cries. All need the outstretched hand of friendship and the assurance that the stresses of their days will ease.

People passing through bereavement, those in deep financial trouble or disappointment and depression, need the knowledge that God can be with them. They need words and acts of understanding which only a warm hand of love can give them.

Helen Good Brenneman, author of *But Not Forsaken, Meditations for the New Mother,* in her volume *My Comforters* offers to others the comfort she received during hospitalization for multiple sclerosis. Her health has continued to fail and she is now in a wheelchair.

One of her doctors reminded her of resources she had to cope with the ailment, things that many others didn't have. She had the prayer support of many congregations, the love of a large Christian community which revealed itself in many forms, as well as the continual living presence of Christ himself. By contrast her partner in the room had only one distant relative and a dog who couldn't be with her.

Helen shares freely the inspiration that strengthened her in her personal struggle with discouragement, weariness, worry, and frustration. Although the problem of suffering has few satisfactory answers, God does give comfort and he uses his children to provide it.

So often people who are sick hear the advice, "Now, don't you worry about a thing!" But any mother, temporarily incapacitated or separated from her family, has an imagination fertile enough to supply her with excellent worry material. Mrs. Brenneman was concerned about many things including her household, her son's first paper route, the mounting medical costs.

A friend sent her a worry-remedy in Philippians 4:6, 7: "Don't worry over anything whatever; tell God every detail of your needs in earnest and thankful prayer, and the peace of God, which transcends human understanding will keep constant guard over your hearts and minds as they rest in Christ Jesus" (Phillips).

Since she couldn't run her household or go along on her son's paper route or even earn the money for the hospital bill, she turned these matters over to God. In her words, "He did a much better job of handling all three concerns than I could have done myself."

God permits some individuals to pass through the dark experiences of life so they can reach back and say to others that God is bigger than any circumstance, any trouble, any adversity, any grief. Their support comes at unexpected moments. Once as I waited for a worship service to start, I engaged in casual conversation with a woman next to me. As we became acquainted she introduced me to her husband sitting behind her in a wheelchair. She explained that about nineteen years ago he had fallen into a silo and broken his back. Since then he had been paralyzed from the waist down. At the time of the accident she had a six-month-old infant and several other children.

Her words thrilled me in a strange way: "Even though I would never want the accident to happen again, I am thankful it did, for it brought us closer to God." Comfort will come through prayer, by tangible gifts, by friendship. Love has many symbols. God comes to us through his Word and through his servants to help us bear suffering, and to bring us hope. Hope is always more important than happiness. I thanked her for her words.

Part
Three

CHAPTER THIRTEEN
When I Am Old

"But it shall come to pass, that at evening time it shall be light" (Zechariah 14:7b).

As a child, I enjoyed reading a story about a house with golden windows. Each evening, the little boy in the story wished he lived in the house with the golden windows, which was across the fields from his lowly home. One day he visited the house and found to his disappointment that the windows were only ordinary glass. Then, looking back toward his own home, he saw its windows gleaming golden in the evening sunset.

As a youngster, whenever I saw golden windows shining in the distance, I had a superior feeling. I felt one up on the little boy: I knew that all windows were only glass. But deep down I wished that the story had never ended, that the windows had always remained golden for him.

When I am old and alone, and the cold mists of life roll through the valleys, so that the sun has difficulty shining through, will the windows in the distance still look golden? What will it be like when I'm much, much older, my hair grayer, my strength weaker, my steps shorter, and my fingers slower to find the typewriter keys—or not able to press them at all? Where will I be living? Here in my little home with my books and papers and typewriter, or in the cold sterility of a convalescent home where windows are always made of glass?

Who will look after me when I'm old? Will there be enough Social Security or other pension money to take care of my financial needs? Will I still have something to do? If so, will I have the energy and desire to do it, or will some social worker help me play bingo and make pot-holders? Will I be healthy and alert or arthritic and forgetful?

At night when the house grows still and only the furnace, fridge, and water softener interrupt my thoughts, checking in to let me know they're still around, I wonder about life alone as a widow in a society that emphasizes the coupled life. I listen to older widows talk about their experiences.

One widow of 68, who now lives in a nursing home, once enjoyed a life filled with happy, rollicking children. She had been a school teacher. Now what was it? "A life of sleep," she described it. "Pretty soon I'll be like Robinson Crusoe; I'll have to put six marks on the wall and cross them with a seventh to keep track of the weeks."

A recent newspaper carried an account of a 91-year-old man who goes to the movies every day like a woman I mentioned in another chapter. Today. To-morrow. The next day. With few exceptions he's spent the last 9,125 days—25 years—at the movies. Each morning after breakfast he leaves his one-room apartment to stroll to a nearby theater. "It gets so boring, I can't even stay home on Sundays," he says. He uses movies to escape old age.

I read of another older person, representative of so many of our aged, who when someone admired the rocking chair in which she was sitting, replied bitterly, "Yes, it's a fine chair and I'm rocking myself to death in it." Must life as an elderly widow be limited to the ruts of a rocker in the rug?

I look around me to see dozens of older widows who live in this community, either alone, in nursing homes, or occasionally with families and friends. I think of my grandmother, who was a widow for more than forty years. We ate many lunches at her modest home. When she tried to speak English with her heavy German accent, we children laughed and she laughed with us. She was always a jolly grandmother. I can see her now in her tall rocking chair, her hands clasped over her ample midriff or smoothing out her long white apron, enjoying the conversation. She enjoyed her rocker because it brought people to her.

I think of other older widows, one whose life has been dedicated to prayer and correspondence with missionaries, who praises the Lord for his goodness every time I meet her. And of one whose timidity, affecting her even when her husband was alive, has now frightened her almost out of life. She waits alone, silently, fearfully, in her little home. Another, now blind, had lived such an outgoing carefree life, that visiting her was a tonic. She talked about her flowers, her reading, her garden, her canning projects. Life was too exciting to yield a moment to bitterness in spite of bouts with cancer, rheumatic fever, and a few other serious illnesses, in addition to blindness. I see also the widow who has retreated from all activity requiring a contribution from her, not realizing that she is pushing life away from her. Her friends whisper to each other that they wish they could find some way of diluting the vinegar in her system.

What hurdles are ahead of me as I walk through old age, possibly alone? I believe that most older people would like to be able to live with courage and meaning at a time when physical and emotional strength may be low. Yet the enemy of courage is fear writ in large letters. It hits the young, particularly the adolescent wavering before young adulthood. It knows especially well how to undermine the old.

Most of us outgrow our childish fears of the bogeyman at the end of the hall. In our day physical courage is seldom put to the test. Few people are called upon to rescue someone from a snowstorm or an angry bear. We usually live without daily fear of our lives, although in some cities many Americans worry about their possessions being stolen, or even about being mugged in the streets.

Yet our age *is* an age of fear. Widows, having lost someone who represented strength and leadership, are particularly prone to domination by it. I am not thinking of the panic that grips the heart when one realizes that an armed robber is trying to get into the house, but the fear that slowly chills the spirit: "Now that my husband is dead, I am completely at the mercy of complex forces and powers intent on making me their slave." Many women come to depend on husbands to take care of all that purrs, roars, clinks, clanks, or rustles. Now the widow must tangle with engines and pipes, plumbers and lawyers, and above all with that unassailable modern giant, the computer. She may lack a basic understanding of how all this equipment and these processes work.

One older widow found herself totally unable to cope with mounds of paper work she was required to complete after her husband's death. She worried about not having filled out some form correctly or on time or with sufficient copies. Computer card by card, she felt forced to give obeisance to a monster who demanded of her more than she could give. I have sensed this same fear of forms and questionnaires on the part of many older widows, and with it their sense of being manipulated: "We answer many questions, but no one actually listens to us anymore."

Some time ago my subscription to a national magazine stopped coming even though, according to my records, it hadn't expired. I wrote several letters to the company, first explaining, then protesting. In the end I gave up, for I couldn't persuade their computer to reinstate what it had no record of. What if some future day all the facts of my life get erased from some important agency's computer tapes?

Though insurance and pension and medical aid papers give the widow anxiety, she may also have to struggle with a kitchen faucet with chronic catarrh. The plumbers say it's not a big enough job for them to handle, but it's too big for her. What about those heating systems and appliances and cars that promised dependable service and ran so smoothly when her husband was alive, but now develop continual aches and pains? One can pray about gossipy neighbors and the salvation of sinners, but what can God do about a dead telephone, her lifeline into the community? At such times, God's interest and power may seem remote. Ralph Nader and his Raiders seem more concerned than God about how well things work. How can a widow learn to live with complexity, mechanical obsolescence, and frequent breakdowns with no handyman around to take care of the problem? Only with grace and humility. One must learn to admit one's needs and accept help from family, friends, agencies, and businesses who are willing to give aid. Pride has never fixed a plugged sink.

The prophet Daniel at the age of eighty was thrust into a lions' den by his enemies. Though the lions crouched menacingly around him, they didn't hurt him. Today older persons get pushed into the lions' den of old age by a society that doesn't know what else to do with them. It retires some before they're ready, shoves some into nursing homes because no one wants to take care of them, forces others to live alone on inadequate pensions. And always the lions of rejection, boredom, and loneliness lurk nearby waiting for the kill. Wintertime friends are hard to find.

As I think about all this, I recognize that no one can retire from life as one can from a career. After the recognition supper for faithful services, after the corsage and the retirement check, life still goes on. And, some older people ask, what for? The widow who has never worked outside the home hasn't retired. She still has many of the same tasks to do that filled her time before her husband's death. But now there are gaping holes in her day. She thinks back to former times, when she and her husband made plans for the week: church activities, friends in for dinner, choir practice, a shopping trip, a visit from the children. Life was full. Every day had some activity planned.

Married or single, some people's main preoccupation is to outwit time. Every day, every moment has to be filled with activity. When the sun sets, we simply shift gears, switch on lights, and continue with other kinds of work. The attitude that time must always be filled moves into old age with us, and being alone makes it more difficult to succeed at this time-consuming task.

Why do human beings work so hard to knock time senseless, to beat it into the ground? The issue lies in our basic attitude toward time. Because time has no reality or substance—we cannot feel it or taste it—we shrink from it and turn to objects, says Abraham J. Heschel. Many adults, he writes, spend their lives bartering their time for the things of space, things that can be seen and handled. When such people get older and can no longer be actively involved in exchanging time for things, they have to face time itself. It becomes a nightmare to them, a thing to be feared.

Further, time has always represented money. Through work, time can be transformed into things to occupy space like cars and shoes and cameras and perfume. In this sense, time can be touched and felt and seen. The widow who no longer can turn time into beautiful objects to be placed about her home may feel defeated.

Another reason why individuals set out to defeat time is that the principle of superefficiency has been drilled into the core of our beings since we were children. Even in church, "redeeming the time" was interpreted to mean "be busy." Become a joiner, attend meetings, knit while someone gives a speech, prepare notes for a lecture while listening to a lecture, read at the doctor's office, write a letter on the bus, jot a memo while answering the phone. No moment must be lost to silence or inactivity. When we become older, when we enter the twilight years, we must unlearn this attitude.

Twilight, for me as a child, was the magic moment before darkness conquered all. It was a time for just being. I pray that my old age will also be like that. Once, human beings lived by the natural rhythms of day and night, spring and fall, winter and summer. They couldn't do anything else. The old hymn "Work for the Night Is Coming" has little meaning for those who don't understand how completely darkness brought the workday to an end in an earlier era. Today technology has upset natural tempos and pushed us into an artificial pace. When the sun sets, the farmer can continue his field work with lights on his tractor. In the house and office and factory, work continues with artificial lights. Time can be manipulated.

Years ago, when day was day and night was night, twilight became that precious time for a few last moments outside before Mother called us in for the night. Frequently at twilight I relaxed in a high-backed rocker with a patchwork cushion, wondering and dreaming about what it would be like when I was grown up. Twilight was a time for finding and listening to the silence within. Soon Father would come home from the store, and we would gather around the oak table in the dining room for our simple meal. Night had begun. Today as soon as the tiniest shadow darkens a corner, someone switches on a light, and our activity goes on. The opportunity to know silence is chased away.

Another reason why time has become our common enemy is that society sees time as the grim reaper of youth. To grow old is to lose time, not to gain it. To be old is to have time run out, as if life is a race with time. To grow old is to move into the country of fear where hope has lost residential privileges. To be old requires one to give up the goals of youth, as if these are the only ones that count.

Most women, at some time in life, consider three goals as all-important: to have an attractive face and body, to gain a husband, and to bear children. Yet these goals all belong to youth. Age creeps up and wrinkles form, the body sags, the hair turns gray, the fresh appeal of youth departs. Children grow up and leave the family home to build their own. When the only goals a woman has are the goals of youth, when youth ends, she may find life emptying also. She may feel that life is over when she has moved past the childbearing years. Life dwindles to waiting for old age and death if she thinks that the young, the ones who are beautiful and clear-skinned, the ones who have families about them, are the achievers.

Those who see old age as an enemy will think of it as a sentence to join hobby clubs and play shuffleboard, to sit in rocking chairs and wait for company and letters. For them, to be old means living on memories instead of dreams. To be old means not counting in the affairs of church and society which may still interest the older widow very much. To be old means withdrawing from the conflict of life to join the spectators. Yet to think of time as the thief of youth is to forget that the natural lot of humankind is to grow older. No one has ever grown younger. If old age is the twilight period before God calls his children home, time is not an enemy.

Only in time do we find out who we are. Only in time do we make a friend. Only in time do we learn to love. Only in time do we meet God. We can retire from none of these activities. "In the whole vast expanse of human history there is only one point of contact with the Lord of human history: the present moment," writes Michel Quoist. "It is through the door of the present moment that God enters into your life, and it is through you that he enters into the life of the world."

Just to be busy is not to be a blessing. Just to kill time is not to live. Just to idealize the past or to wait for the future is not to be holy. God meets us only in the present moment—this moment of grace—when we take time for him, whether we're young or old. If time is our ally, and not our enemy, it means we must always keep growing and learning and serving as we are able.

I enjoy reading accounts of older people's lives; for their accomplishments confuse the definition of old age. Is it at sixty-five to seventy-five? I doubt it. Myrtie L. Elmer, a semi-invalid who had lost her last living relative, was seventy-five when her pastor advised her to record her spiritual experiences on paper as therapy for her soul. For the next ten years she kept a diary (published upon her death at eighty-five as *Conversations with God*). Reading it is a stirring challenge in understanding the purpose of physical suffering and loneliness.

A radio commentator mentioned a woman of seventy-eight with failing eyesight who found she could no longer write letters to children and friends. She piled the words one on top of the others. With the help of the Institute for the Blind, she learned to type. At eighty she was still typing her missives of love with very few mistakes.

"I guess I'm getting old," complained an older friend, rubbing her arthritic knee with one hand. She was well past God's allotted three score years and ten. Actually, after she had passed her twentieth birthday, the aging process had already set in. It doesn't start when the first grey hair gleams some fateful morning, or when the first grandchild is added to the family tree, or even when you're asked to move on to the next age group in Bible study classes. Once we've reached the peak of youth we're all growing old together, scientific research tells us. We reach the peak of our intelligence and the maturity of our bodies at about twenty. From then on we begin to slow down.

Does that mean we aren't as good as we once were? No, the slowing down process is mostly in our reactions. The intelligence of an older person isn't any less than that of a young person. The older person should be wiser and have more mature judgment because of experience.

The older widow must be convinced she is never too old to continue learning. She may have to give herself more time, but that isn't because she's old. As one person commented, "It isn't the person who's worn out, but her early training." Some of her education may have become obsolete.

I would like to encourage any retired widow to try a second vocation, or even a first one—if she found her main satisfaction in the home during her husband's lifetime. Hopefully, she has many advantages the recent graduate may not have: stability, reliability, good judgment. Our society is getting away from the idea that the person who switches careers in midstream is fickle. I hope we'll eventually also get away from the idea that a person's usefulness is past once he or she reaches old age. Before they find their rocking chairs too comfortable, older people should catch the appeal of the creative life open to them in a second career, possibly even overseas. Older people still have considerable physical strength. They are intellectually keen and capable of learning new skills. They should know something about getting along with others. Repeatedly, they have proven that studies aren't beyond them. One summer the oldest student on the university campus where I was studying was seventy. In the spring of 1975 I taught a short course in writing memoirs to a group of persons over age sixty. They were an alert, eager group of students, and the oldest among the group was over eighty!

A widow with a satisfactory retirement income should seriously consider service under some mission board or similar organization. If she has spent twenty-five successful years in a paid profession, why not consider another ten in a vocation without pay: hostess or housemother in a mission hostel, teacher, or receptionist? Most gerontologists agree that it's better to work at some worthwhile activity upon retirement than to center one's attention only on superficial activities, such as entertainment.

Efforts to bring older people back into the academic world by offering them an opportunity to attend college at reduced or no fees is gaining support and should be encouraged. A person with a growing mind is seldom lonely. One woman in Missouri, whose marriage side-tracked her educational plans years ago, received her high school diploma at the age of seventy-eight. "I don't envy anybody their clothes or their money or their looks, but when they know things, I envy them," she said. Old age won't frighten or bore that kind of person.

For the much older widow, after her *second* career has ended, life may retreat once again. At times she may not have much strength to use her hands and feet. What then?

It used to be that the older people of a society were the chief links with the wisdom of the past, providing the present generation with the security of a fixed pattern of doing things. They gave society continuity. Younger members of the family went to the older ones for advice and information. Mothers taught their daughters how to make butter "come" on a hot day, how to treat a child sick with croup, how to make soap. Mother's recipe for poundcake was handed down to each daughter and to daughters' daughters.

Our modern era has changed this way of educating the young. Women's magazines have, to a large extent, replaced the practical wisdom and advice of the older women of our society. They set the example of how to dress, how to get a man and keep him, how to cook, how to decorate our homes, how to bring up children, how to help in community affairs. We get our household hints by the lineal yard from Heloise. Other nationwide columnists give us balm for lacerated emotions with their words of wit and sometimes wisdom. We snip and file recipes of other cultures from magazines on the super-market shelves. Dr. Benjamin Spock tells us how to bring up our children. Grandmother has been shoved out of the picture.

Yet when I turn to the Scriptures, I read that "the old women should be reverent in their behavior . . . They should be examples of the good life, so that the younger women may learn to love their husbands and their children, to be sensible and chaste, home lovers, kindhearted and willing to adapt themselves to their husbands—a good advertisement for the Christian faith" (Titus 2:4, 5 Phillips). So the older woman still has a work to do. After she has been a learner, and a doer, she still must be a teacher.

Young people rushing headlong into a pleasure-crazed, fast-living world need to know that life is hard, but that it is good if lived with God. They need to know that marriage is no roller-coaster heaven but a difficult and demanding relationship with many rich and satisfying experiences. Some young mothers expect that love, patience, and understanding of husband and children will come naturally to them. These lessons must be learned, sometimes painfully, often slowly. Older women can help teach them. How are they taught? Not in a formal classroom but over the back fence, while helping to care for small children, or wherever women get together.

Nothing is more beautiful and appealing than the serene dignity and joyous attitude of a mature older woman who faces life with trust in God. Such an attitude is contagious. Paul wrote that if older women failed in the task of teaching younger women, the Word of God was open to reproach. If Christianity fails at the basic level of society, the home, how can it work at other levels? With our homes facing a continuing time of troubled transition, we need mature women ready to share the values they have gained in a lifetime with God. We may need to make more opportunity for real communication between older and younger women in our crowded, busy world. I know there are times when older women are happy to get away from "baby talk," but there are also times when younger women need someone who can speak openly to them from the perspective of years.

Margaret Mead states that one lesson needed today is how to stand change. Women in all age groups today are facing greater changes than women have ever faced before. When should a woman move along with societal changes, when hold back? From the aged, we can learn how to handle change and still maintain contact with a Redeemed God. Older women, single, widowed, or married, are to be a spiritual link between God and young women. They are to be a steadying influence, a source of encouragement and strength. With one hand in God's, older widows are to reach out with the other to young mothers: "I understand what you are going through. God helped me. He will also help you."

I believe I must learn one other thing before I take my place with the aged. It is acceptance of physical aging as one of the facts of life. There may come a time when I must be willing to relinquish all doing and simply accept the being. Even then I don't advocate resignation from living, but an acceptance of the natural rhythms of life. The adolescent is expected to get an education and prepare for life. Young adulthood is the time for working and achieving, middle-age the time for settling in and strengthening what has already been begun. Then comes old age, a beautiful time, in which one is no longer expected to perform or to produce. One can simply be.

I enjoy visiting the community where my parents live, a retirement center on the West Coast. The weather gently accommodates the aches and pains of the aged. Masses of brightly-colored flowers cheer my eyes, those of a Kansas dweller accustomed to their dearth in midsummer. In the background, mountains hover over the community like a nanny guarding her charges. As I tour their shopping center, I notice how the community caters to its special citizens, the elderly, by attitude and action. Drivers watch for the many pedestrians taking their daily walk to town for a few groceries.

One of the phenomena of our time is the clustering of the elderly in the pleasant valleys and plains. It seems necessary, yet as a result our society loses—for the young lose contact with the old.

The other evening I looked over the large congregation at a union service, noticing the predominance of snowy heads. My own community is also a retirement center. I contemplated the faithfulness of this group in church attendance, in giving, in praying, in doing—for the Lord and in other types of service. For most of them the time has come simply to *be* for the Lord. Many of these older persons, widowed and married, have found healing from life's sorrows and are free from the strain of striving to get ahead in life. An attitude of relinquishment is a final step before one moves gracefully to the other side. It makes death easier to face.

Keith Miller in *The Becomers* points out that we are all empire builders in our social, vocational, and church worlds, continually looking for places of security. But

Christ expects Christians to turn loose our securities and reach with faith toward new opportunities. All that we have clutched over the years to build ourselves up—our abilities, status, possessions—these must be turned over to God as we continue our pilgrimage. Such relinquishment, according to Pierre Teilhard de Chardin, is the perfect preparation for death. At the end of life, the Christian who has surrendered all encumbrances to God has only to turn over his or her body before joining the Creator.

Is such relinquishment possible? I read again Myrtie L. Elmer's account of her last years before her death. She was crippled with arthritis. Later she broke a hip. Her eyesight gradually left her. Her remaining brother died, leaving her totally alone in the world. Her solitary state puzzled her. "Shall I make new friends? Shall I find new work to do?"

Her spiritual journal reflected both her certitudes and her doubts: "I cannot grasp, except to a very limited degree, the meaning which Christ's life and death should have for us. But I do know that it has become very real to me that Christ is divine and that He is *ruler* in the spiritual realm."

As time edged along, she dared to ask questions like, "What do others do when they face approaching blindness?" She assured herself that nothing could separate her from the love of God. After she broke her hip, death was not yet to be her lot. She made the entry: "Was it that I was so ill-prepared to enter His presence? Is there some service which He wants me to render Him still on earth?"

Each added year, the pages of her journal were filled with recordings of doubts, pain, and discomfort, but also of sustained trust. She quoted Howard Thurman's *Deep Is the Hunger:* "Life is alive, and every tiny rootlet and every tiny nerve cell charged with the energy of the eternal. Old age, sickness, fading of the powers is fought inch by inch all the way to the grave." "Hallelujah," she commented.

Though she could do no work, earn no money, she thanked God for his disciplines along the road of life as well as for joy. Occasionally she contemplated death and what it would be like "when time ticks itself away in these days and nights, and the familiar life as we know it comes to an end." In her eighty-fourth year she wrote that "growing old has lost its terrors and my greatest hope is that through each remaining day of earthly life the Lord will give me strength to do what He wishes me to do."

She gave tribute to those lonely years as a great opportunity for quiet meditation. After her retirement from teaching, she had found opportunities for creative work, but when the handicaps of old age and its infirmities increased, she used "quiet periods for meditation and prayer, and just aloneness, or possibly more truly for what Nicodemus in *Treasures of Darkness* calls 'at-one-ment,' to make the personality whole. God listens, and I am alone with him."

As her health steadily deteriorated, she came to deal more specifically with death in her journal. "Am I afraid to die?" "Shall I be when the time comes?" She recognized that the experience of transition from one world to the other must come for all, and that any kind of change produces fear. But underneath she had the conviction that her love for Christ and faith in him were greater than fear.

On May 26, 1959, she wrote: "I am old, physically infirm, and lame. No close relatives live near me. Much of the time there is pain, and minor annoyances are like besetting sins—ever present. But praise be unto God, when the skies seem heaviest, by His grace there breaks through the gladdest knowledge in the world, the blessed, blessed realization that there is still the 'Presence of God' in this troubled world and in our lives."

She died at the age of eighty-five. One of her last entries was "I rejoice because the Lord is my shepherd."

In the television show "All in the Family," bigot Archie Bunker encounters a couple of oldsters who have found each other in a retirement home. The older man tosses a remark at Archie which staggers him and which reflects the thinking of many people, "Sonny, don't grow too old." How unlike Robert Browning's words:

> Grow old along with me!
> The best is yet to be,
> The last of life, for which the first was made:
> Our times are in His hand
> Who saith, "A whole I planned,
> Youth shows but half; trust God: see all, nor be afraid!"

Widowhood. Old age. A combination that looks like sure calamity.

Widowhood. Old age. Faith in God. A combination that assures that at "evening time it shall be light." The windows across the Jordan will not only look golden but will be of pure gold.

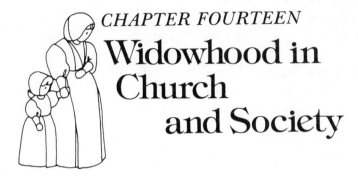

CHAPTER FOURTEEN
Widowhood in Church and Society

"And she answered, I am indeed a widow woman, and mine husband is dead" (2 Samuel 14:5)

To help me understand my role, I have undertaken some helpful studies on the status of widows in Bible times and later in church life. I recommend this as a project to all widows troubled by the burdensome image thrust upon them by church and society. The early status of widows still affects modern-day widows, and does so needlessly. Tradition is a strong molder of roles.

The word *widow* derives from the Latin *vidua* (widow) and *dividere,* meaning to divide or separate. From early times, a widow was not only separated from her husband through death, but separated from society because of her new role. She became a member of a group set apart: "and the widows."

Modern feminists of both secular society and the Christian church have been attempting to show that a woman who has no power or position in the economic structure of society lacks an identity. This is true also for men, but because in the past more women than men have lacked economic strength, women's actions (and words written and spoken by women) have not been valued as highly as those coming from men. Poverty accounts in large part for the status of widows on the bottom rung of the social ladder in Old Testament times. Attitudes toward the widow were often based on her lack of financial independence.

OLD TESTAMENT

In Old Testament times, the notion of the inferiority of women seems to have been generally accepted in Hebrew culture. Women were expected to be subordinate and submissive, with their sphere of activity confined mainly to the home. A woman was expected to marry, to raise children to perpetuate her husband's name, and to encourage him in his relationship to Jehovah. In that patriarchal society a woman found her identity in relationship to the male members of the family. She began life as a daughter (Merab, daughter of Saul), moved to the home of her husband and became his wife (Elisheba, wife of Aaron) and mother of male children (Hannah, mother of Samuel). Readers of the Old Testament have learned to recognize and accept these women by this identity. When a woman was widowed, she lost her identity in relationship to some man and often returned to her father's home. Naomi, after the death of her husband and sons, returned home to Judah and encouraged her two daughters-in-law also to return to their homes. She wanted them to stay in their native land of Moab.

Some widows in the Old Testament are identified only by the locality from which they came.

Various degrees of status existed among Hebrew women, with the top category, of course, the married woman with sons. She was Israel's most respected woman. Childlessness was considered a deep affliction and the woman's fault. At the bottom of the social ladder were the female slaves who were at the complete command of their master. Rebekah's nurse may have been a slave, given to Rebekah as part of her dowry when she left home (Genesis 24:59).

The concubine's lot was little better than a slave's. Sometimes she was a slave, but the man to whom she belonged couldn't dispose of her when he tired of her. He either had to keep her, or let her go free, or permit her relatives to redeem her. King Solomon was known for his many concubines.

The term "servants" in the Old Testament sometimes includes the slaves of the household. On occasion they were servants as we think of them, but rarely were they wage earners who were free to come and go. Sarah gave Abraham her servant Hagar to bear him a son. The master of the household was expected to protect and provide for the servants as he did other members in his care. Some slaves filled important and responsible positions and received the dignity that went with these positions, as, for example, Joseph in Potiphar's household (Genesis 39:1-5). Naaman's wife had a servant girl, who was a slave captured in battle.

On another level in Hebrew society were the harlots. Although the Israelites were clearly warned against the evils of prostitution, prostitutes actively solicited customers (Leviticus 21:7; Deuteronomy 23:18). A harlot named Rahab helped the Israelite spies who came to investigate the land.

Even in those days not all women married, so in another category were those who remained single, such as Miriam, sister of Moses. Jephthah's daughter was forced to remain single (Judges 11:34, 35, 40). Also, some women were divorced and others shared their husbands with other wives. Polygamy was practiced, and many of the patriarchs had more than one wife (Jacob had Leah and Rachel).

As I examined in greater detail the role of the widow in Old Testament times, I found that it was frequently an unhappy one, especially for the widow who in the days of her marriage had been unable to provide her husband with children, particularly sons. Widows are usually mentioned as a separate class, grouped with strangers, the poor, and the fatherless—an oppressed group. The death of her husband set the widow into an entirely different social and economic group. She clothed herself in sackcloth, let her hair hang loose, and did not anoint her face (Judith 10:3, 4; 16:8). She was identified to society by the way she dressed. Tamar, determined that her rights to motherhood under Levirate law not be denied her, removed her widow's garments and put on a veil, pretending to be a harlot. Later she returned to her widow's garments.

With the death of her husband, who during her lifetime had been her economic support, the widow moved out of regular economic circles. Frequently, because she had no means of self-support, she became a burden to other people. The laws of inheritance awarded her husband's estate to his male kinsmen if there were no children. She herself returned to her father's home or was supported by adult children, if she had any. She might also become part of her husband's family group, an arrangement made possible through Levirate law. In that case she would be given to the next oldest son as his wife, so that she might bear children. The first son born of this union bore her husband's name (Deuteronomy 25:5, 6). If the brother refused to accept the widow, renouncing thereby his right to her estate, she was to take off his sandal and spit in his face, saying, "Thus we requite the man who will not build up his brother's family."

Tamar was the wife of Judah's eldest son. When he died, according to custom, Tamar was entitled to bear children by the next oldest brother, who was Onan. He refused to impregnate her because he knew "the seed should not be his," so he ejaculated on the ground instead. When he also died, Judah advised Tamar to remain as a widow in her father's house until his third son Shelah grew up. This she did.

However, when Shelah was mature, she was not given to him as his wife, so on hearing that her father-in-law was going to Timnath to shear sheep, she played the harlot with him (Genesis 38:19). Judah, thinking she was a common prostitute, had intercourse with her in exchange for the payment of a kid from the flock. He gave her his seal and cord and staff as pledge for payment. When Judah sent the kid in payment, he couldn't find the prostitute. Tamar conceived and was about to be burned as a prostitute by the men of the place, but at the crucial moment she produced the pledges of Judah's payment. Judah recognized them, saying, "She is more in the right than I am because I did not give her to my son Shelah." In due time, she delivered twins.

If a widow had children, she became the overseer of money left to them. Because widows were usually untrained in the ways of the financial world, they easily became the prey of men ready to grab what means they had, or, if she was in financial difficulty, eager to lend her money at high rates of interest. Some widows accumulated many debts because of their financial ineptitude. The woman with two sons (2 Kings 4:1-7) came to Elisha to complain that her creditors were planning to take her boys away as slaves because she had no money to pay them. It must have been common practice to maltreat the widow and the fatherless, for the Old Testament contains many admonitions against doing so, even to warning against taking her cloak as surety for a debt (Deuteronomy 24:17).

Widowhood, like barrenness, was considered a shame and reproach in Israel (Isaiah 54:1-5). In a messianic prophecy, Isaiah admonished Zion, "the barren woman," to sing aloud over the prospect of having "more sons than the married woman." To "the widow" he said: "It is time to forget the shame of your younger days and remember no more the reproach of your widowhood; for your husband is your maker, whose name is the Lord of Hosts" (Isaiah 54:4, 5 NEB).

Like all women, widows in the Old Testament were considered on the same level as things and cattle which the men owned. The women of Midian (Numbers 31:9), after their husbands were killed in battle, were taken as captives by the Israelite army. With their children, cattle, flocks, and other possessions, these women were taken to Moses and Eleazar. Moses was upset because the women hadn't been killed with the others, and instead had been brought home as spoils of battle. Because they were members of a people who had "caused the children of Israel, through the counsel of Balaam, to commit trespass against the Lord," Moses ordered all the widows and their male dependents to be killed. All the virgins (32,000 of them) were saved and given to the Israelites as wives.

The image of widows that emerges from the Old Testament is that of a group of women isolated in their poverty, subject to oppression and injustice, whose cries often were not heard, and who in their loneliness and abject need became a symbol of all oppressed and needy. The prophet Jeremiah likens the children of Israel in exile to a widow:

> How solitary lies the city, once so full of people!
> Once great among nations, now become a widow;
> Once queen among provinces, now put to forced labor.
> Bitterly she weeps in the night, tears run down her cheeks;
> She has no one to bring her comfort among all that love her. (Lamentations 1:1 NEB).

Jeremiah speaks of the Lord punishing those who cast him off by making widows among them (Jeremiah 15:8; 18:21). In sending Elijah to the widow of Zarephath, God sent the prophet to the kind of person whose economic resources were very slight. Living with her became a test of Elijah's faith that God would provide, and a test of the widow's faith that, as she gave of her meager means, both

227

she and the man of God would have enough to eat. Each day God provided sufficient oil and meal to supply their needs.

Because a widow's economic and emotional needs were often so acute, and because men set her aside as a useless individual, throughout the Old Testament God speaks of himself as the widow's champion (Psalm 68:5; 146:9; Proverbs 15:25). The Lord is the one who defends the poor and the orphans (Psalm 82:3; Isaiah 1:17). He is a swift witness against any who oppress the children of a widow (Malachi 3:5; Psalm 10:14; Zechariah 7:10). Because he is on the widow's side, those against widows and the fatherless are in danger of judgment (Deuteronomy 27:19; 24:17; Proverbs 23:10; Jeremiah 22:3; Ezekiel 22:7; Psalm 94:6; Malachi 3:5; Isaiah 10:2). To hurt a widow or orphan was a crime (Exodus 22:22, 23; Deuteronomy 14:29; 24:17, 19; 26:12; 27:19; Job 24:3; Psalm 68:5; Proverbs 15:25). Again and again the Israelites were admonished to show their mercifulness by the way they treated the fatherless, the aliens, the widows (Isaiah 1:17; Exodus 22:21, 22; Malachi 3:5).

To make allowance for the needs of aliens, orphans, and widows, the Israelites were instructed to leave on the ground any grain not picked up the first time around a field, as well as the gleanings of olive trees and grapevines. Ruth was one of the gleaners in a field when Boaz spotted her.

At the end of every third year the Israelites were to tithe all their produce and leave it in the settlements so that the Levites, aliens, orphans, and widows in their midst could come and eat their fill. If they did this, the

Lord would bless them in everything to which they set their hand.

The rights of widows were few. In addition to the right to motherhood under the Levirate law, widows were entitled to make a vow which was considered valid. The vow of a married woman had no validity in a court of law (Numbers 30:9). The widow also had the right to worship together with the rest of the community: with the sons and daughters, male and female slaves, the Levites, and the orphans.

And so the widow lived within the Hebrew community, usually without economic strength, lonely, oppressed, recognized by "widow's weeds," a symbol of the un-protected helpless members of society whose champion was the Lord.

NEW TESTAMENT: THE GOSPELS

The New Testament image of the widow does not appear to have changed much from Old Testament times: she was still poor. As the Levirate laws of marriage broke down, widows were left to make their own way and, as a result, became objects of charity. At the time of Christ, the Jews had established a fund in the temple to provide for the needs of widows and orphans (2 Maccabees 3:10). Few widows appear in the record of Jesus's life on earth, though he drew attention to the widow who threw all her money into the temple coffers—two mites (Mark 12:41-44). He talked about Pharisees who loved to go about in long clothing, to be saluted in the market place, who chose the best seats in the synagogues, who made long prayers for the sake of appearance, yet who devoured widows' houses (Matthew 23:14; Luke 20:47).

Jesus restored to life the son of a widow of Nain (Luke 7:12), the first person he raised from the dead. When Jesus came to the gate of the city, he saw a dead man being carried out, the only son of a widow. The story doesn't indicate whether the many townspeople with her were relatives or paid mourners. The widow didn't appeal to Jesus for help, but when he saw her, he had compassion upon her and told her to stop crying. The young man was restored to life and to his mother.

An importunate widow (Luke 18:3, 5) appears in one of Jesus' parables as an example of persistence in prayer. This widow had an adversary or opponent who she thought was treating her unfairly. She came to the judge, begging for justice. For a long time he refused her, but in the end he agreed to her request because she was so insistent.

A widow was the first person to proclaim Jesus as the Christ. Anna, the prophetess, stands out in the New Testament as a widow who had gained victory over domination by her own emotional and materialistic needs. She spent her days and nights serving God with fasting and prayer. Luke described her as the daughter of Phanuel of the tribe of Aser. She was old, although not all scholars are agreed whether she lived with her husband for seven years and then was widowed for eighty-four years, or whether she was eighty-four years old at the time she saw the Christ-child. She apparently knew something about Old Testament prophecy, for coming "in that instant gave thanks likewise unto the Lord, and spake of him to all them that looked for redemption in

Jerusalem" (Luke 2:38). She was able to tell those who were in the temple at the same time as Mary and Joseph that their child was the one for whom all Israel had been waiting.

Some scholars believe that Mary, the mother of John Mark, was a widow. The sisters Mary and Martha managed a household in which their brother Lazarus also lived. It seems unlikely that all three members of this family never married. Possibly Martha, the older of the two sisters, was a widow and Mary had never married. They were financially well off, for Mary later poured a pound of costly ointment of spikenard (John 12:3) on the feet of Jesus. We learn in Mark 14:5 that the ointment might have been sold for 300 *denarii,* a workingman's wage for a year.

Numerous women—married, widowed, and unmarried—are mentioned in the Gospels as having a fairly close relationship with Jesus. Yet he never openly referred to their marital status, whatever it may have been—with the exception of the Samaritan woman, whom he met by the well. He mentioned her many husbands for a purpose because it involved a moral issue. Then he turned her into a proclaimer of the Good News to the people of her village.

In the Gospels I found that Christ's relationship with women moved away from the Old Testament concept that to be unmarried was a reproach and a shame. He gave these first women to come to him, whatever their marital status, a purpose in life that went beyond seeking answers to their personal needs only in the context of marriage.

231

APOSTOLIC TIMES

When Jewish widows who had been supported from the temple fund were converted, and joined the Christian community, their temple support was presumably cut off. Thus in the early church, Christians found themselves responsible for a large group of widows who had no other means of support—no Social Security or pension plan or the skills or opportunity to take on a job. Jewish widows were probably among the group taken care of in the general distribution following Pentecost, until some Greek converts complained that *their* widows weren't being treated fairly. The complaint led to organization of the diaconate in the church, but not to organization of the widows. Even here, widows stand out as a group with specific economic needs and as individuals in need of an advocate because of their powerless situation.

The story of Dorcas confirms that widows stood out as a group characterized by their penury in the Christian community. Because the widows had no husbands to support them, Dorcas, who may have been a wealthy widow, made them clothing. They had no way of repaying her kindness except with gratitude. After the apostle Peter restored her to life, he called in the congregation, or God's people, "and the widows" (Acts 9:36-43).

The only passage in the New Testament dealing substantially with widows is 1 Timothy 5:3-16, which suggests that in apostolic times there were widows, and then there were "real" widows. The issue that the apostle Paul was discussing was once again the economic relief of widows. They had material needs that had to be met by the household of God. In a close study of the passage, it becomes clear that a widow was to be supported first by her children and grandchildren (v. 4). If she had no children, her support was to be provided by other relatives (v. 8). Anyone who did not take care of a widow in the family was considered worse than an infidel and had denied the faith. Verse 16 seems to indicate that if a woman had widows in her family, she was to take care of them herself. Lastly, if all other means of support were not available to the widow, the church (God's community) was required to provide for her needs. She was not to be left without support of some kind.

Although most Bible scholars agree that the church was to provide for the daily needs of women who had no personal means of support, they debate strongly whether an actual order of widows existed in the early church. To admit to this gives women a place in the ecclesiastical structure of the church. Paul speaks about "real" widows, those who are alone in the world, who have all their hopes set on God, and who regularly attend meetings for prayer and worship.

In contrast to this type of widow was the "merry widow," who had experienced in addition to her husband's death a decline of her own spiritual life. This type of widow lived for selfish pleasures and was not to be included on the role or list of widows. The "real widow" was required to be sixty years of age, yet it seems difficult to believe that a young widow with children to support would be denied church help. The widows with the greatest need would obviously be those with young children.

In addition to age requirements, a second stipulation for widows to be enrolled in this special group was that they shouldn't have remarried. Special credit was attributed to women who didn't remarry, as the prophetess Anna apparently refrained from doing. Further, they should have maintained a reputation for motherliness, hospitality, humility, and good works while their husband was alive.

The issue in this passage is why widows were enrolled or listed in church records. If it was only for financial support, why the age limit? Was the enrolling for the sake of establishing a special ministry for them? Some scholars are sure that the enrolling was indicative of "certain duties the church required" of them because they could be depended on to devote themselves wholly to a spiritual ministry. Other scholars disagree as heartily. It has also been suggested that widows may have been the church's official hosts, because of their experience in hospitality while married; yet it's hard to accept this idea because guests aren't usually sent to homes that can least afford to be hospitable.

Another suggestion is that the widows enrolled in the church lists had no specific tasks assigned to them and they regulated their own work, since they were under no masculine supervision. Because they were poor, prayer and fasting were their main tasks. They may also have had a part in going from house to house collecting money for the needs of the church or in helping to care for orphan children. Admittedly, the actual ministry of the widows on church lists is not clear.

What is clear is that widows at this point in church history were given a place of respect or special recognition and that they were the first group of women to be dignified in any way as a body. Widowhood was no longer a reproach or a shame as it once had been. Widows, though poor, could expect the loving support of the community of faith without feeling humiliated. They were part of the family of God and something was expected of them in the spiritual work of the church. In the 1 Timothy passage, Paul advised younger widows to remarry, although in 1 Corinthians 7:8, as the church matured, he advised widows to remain unmarried in order to serve the church more fully.

EARLY CHURCH

Charles C. Ryrie traces the history of widowhood in the early church in *The Place of Women in the Church*. Although some Jewish Christian widows sought remarriage, widows had to be supported from a church fund. But the church gave them more than economic support. It provided an opportunity for a ministry of prayer. Later this work was enlarged to meet other needs of members of the congregations, although details are difficult to construct from extant writings. Throughout this period, duties were not prescribed for enrollment in a group of widows.

Ignatius, writing to Polycarp, said, "Let not widows be neglected. After the Lord be thou their protector." To Christians of Smyrna he wrote, "I salute the households of my brethren with their wives and children, and the virgins who are called widows." The meaning of this passage is disputed by scholars. Some believe that young virgins had become part of the group of widows, and others that the word is used metaphorically, referring to widows as a group who were virgin in body and spirit, or "virgins a second time," "virgins in God's sight."

About A.D. 115, Polycarp, bishop of Smyrna, wrote to the Philippians about the function of widows as interceding for all. He referred to them (with institutionalized groups such as bishops, deacons, and presbyters) as the "altar of God." From this it seems clear that there existed a recognized ecclesiastical order of widows who carried some significant responsibility in the church. Whether they ever constituted an order in the church to the same extent as that of the deaconesses is not clear.

In some areas, mature women of good character, who had teaching functions or responsibilities for preparing women for baptism or communion, or who acted as doorkeepers or ushers in the church, were absorbed into the same group, even if they weren't widows. The "presiding widow," writes Elsie Thomas Culver in *Women in the World of Religion,* was approximately what her title implies, a powerful woman in the church. Her work and that of deaconesses often overlapped.

In the time of the Apologists (i.e., the second century), documents show clearly that virgins, widows, and servants were kept distinct from one another by the churches. But regardless of these distinctions, special offices for women in the churches died out within the next few centuries.

About A.D. 250, there were more than 1,500 widows on the roll to be supported by the church at Rome. They formed a prominent group in that church which was noted as having "many praiseworthy widows." During the third century, the ministry of women was evidently felt to be basic in a newly organized assembly. In addition to intercession, their ministry seems to have been officially enlarged to caring for sick women and receiving revelations. During this time, widows were apparently divided into two classes, those who were enrolled in an order and those who were not, the only qualification for enrollment being age, ten years younger than that specified in Timothy's epistle. Both groups, enrolled and unenrolled, were to receive support from the church. They were to fast and pray for sick and distressed members, to visit them, and to lay their hands on them.

In this century, the church fathers spoke frequently of the widows, sometimes with great approval. Tertullian was against their teaching or baptizing, so one can assume that some widows had moved into that area of work. Tertullian wrote of a repentant adulterer who was brought into the church "before the widows, before the elders." In his congregation, specific regulations governed admittance into the category of widows: married only once, mothers, over sixty years of age. Although he did not accept an open public ministry for these women, he approved of their receiving revelations from the Lord and of their reporting to the leaders after the congregation was dismissed. Obviously, Christian women, including widows, were taking a recognized place in public life during this period of church history. Ryrie writes, "During the first and second century the widow was the prominent [female] figure in the church."

In the Apostolic Church Order, variously dated, but believed to be written about A.D. 300, widows again appear in a list that includes bishops, presbyters, readers, and deacons. Some scholars aren't ready to admit that inclusion of deaconesses and widows in this listing means a distinct order for them. They do agree that virgins, widows, and servants were three groups of women kept distinct by the early church, with widows the most prominent group. They were expected to serve the church primarily through prayer.

The Apostolic Constitution of the fourth century reads: "Let the widow mind nothing but to pray for those that give and for the whole church, and when she is asked anything by anyone let her not easily answer, excepting questions concerning the faith and righteousness and hope in God . . . She is to sit at home, sing, pray, read, watch and fast, speak to God continually in songs and hymns."

Ryrie suggests how deaconesses may have developed from the group of widows in the church. As the ministry of widows began to expand to include other things beside intercession, deaconesses were chosen from the order of widows to devote themselves especially to the task of ministering to the sick. A regulation of the fourth century Apostolic Constitution says, "But let a deaconess be a pure virgin; but if not, then a widow once married, faithful, and honourable."

During the first few centuries after Christ's ministry on earth, widows were outstanding figures in the church. Because of their prominence, a trend developed toward asceticism among young women, resulting in an increasing group of virgins in the church, and an acceptance of celibacy as a higher status than marriage. Special church offices for women (deaconesses, widows, or virgins) died out in a few centuries. Not until the Middle Ages, when the conventual movement developed in relationship to monasticism, did women appear again as a significant group in the church.

It is clear then, that during these first centuries Christianity moved one step above Judaism not only by providing widows with material support, but—like Christ—by offering them the privilege and opportunity of some type of spiritual service in the church. Prayer was expected of them, perhaps the rearing of orphan children, and the visiting of the sick. They didn't have to wait in the shadows for death to overcome them as it had their husbands. In other words, as Ryrie says, "Whatever ministry widows may have performed at the very beginning was not performed because they were widows but simply because they were women." They were enabled to move beyond widowhood. The development of the order of widows later on was not to make them an ecclesiastical order but to aid the total ministry of the church.

MIDDLE AGES

Very little is known about the life and work of women, including widows, during the next few centuries. Widows as a distinct group within the church disappeared. Invading Teutonic hordes from the north brought about the fall of the Roman Empire in A.D. 476, changing the life of Europe and with it the life of the church. The period referred to as the Dark Ages was characterized by surges of barbarians sacking, pillaging, and forcing their uncivilized customs upon the lands they overran. "The whole world is sinking into ruin," wrote St. Jerome in this period.

Men were away trying to protect their country from invaders. Women remained at home. In an unsettled society, survival of self and family took precedence. The destitute, particularly the widows, orphans, and aged turned to the church for help. Many wealthy women also gave their property to the church and took refuge in cloisters. Convent life gave women a status, security, and opportunity for self-development not available elsewhere. Parents got rid of surplus daughters in the same way.

The monasteries, which began as a male movement, did much to preserve religion, learning, and social stability in Europe when these values seemed to be disappearing. In convents, women found opportunity for religious vocations denied them in the church. Here a woman could study, learn, teach, and enjoy a high level of cultural life in art, music, drama, or literature as well as perform a ministry. Capable women, deprived of their traditional orders in the churches (deaconesses, widows, virgins), formed lay associations to care for the sick, orphaned, and widowed.

As plundering barbarians continued to sweep down on western Europe, kings found their strength depleted and turned to the lords for assistance, sometimes giving land in return for military aid. The lord demanded of his lesser lords or vassals loyalty and a supply of soldiers in time of battle in exchange for a fief or tract of land. Peasants or serfs had to go to war in exchange for protection and a small piece of land to farm.

The feudal system had a powerful effect upon the legal position of women. Because a woman couldn't meet the requirements of fighting for an overlord in his battles, her right to hold land was held in question. A young girl who inherited land from her father, or a widow who inherited land from her husband, had a hard time holding it, for the overlord demanded and could force her to marry in order to get his right of military service. The widow and her land and her children were frequently given by the king or overlord to whomever he pleased.

Many women accepted this situation as part of their lot, realizing they couldn't survive without a husband to defend their land. Charlemagne (768-814), on his return from war in Spain, married en masse all the widows of the knights who had died there, thereby inheriting all the land the knights had owned.

During this period, attempts were made to lay down a minimum age at which a girl could be married (twelve years). Marriage became a function rather than a relationship for companionship. Although we may find such an early age dismaying, in fixing it at twelve the church was resisting even earlier marriages. Some girls were being married at the age of five to bring together military strength and land.

Many marriages were arranged during this time. As a result, although the body of the woman became the property of the husband, her mind often escaped in romantic love with a lover, a generally accepted practice. A Code of Love of the Twelfth Century with thirty-one points set forth guidelines for extramarital affairs and widowhood.

The Crusades of the Middle Ages also severely affected the lot of women. Hundreds of thousands of men journeyed to the Holy Land to win it from the Turkish "infidels." Hundreds of women were left unprovided for and without opportunity of marriage. Many others were widowed when their husbands were killed in battle. During the twelfth century the Beguine movement developed to alleviate the many needs resulting from the Crusades, the Black Death, and famines, floods, and droughts that swept through the continent. These groups of women lived and worshiped together, devoting themselves to deeds of charity and service but without formal monastic vows. Lambert le Begue of Liege spent his entire fortune founding a cloister and church for the widows and orphans of crusaders. At the beginning of the Beguine movement (1180), many single women and widows living in the lowlands of western Europe devoted themselves to prayer and good works. They lived on the edge of towns where they could easily help those in need. At first the women lived alone in their own homes, later in small groups. If they were wealthy, they kept servants. Each group of women was complete in itself and established its own program of service. They accepted no charity, but earned their living by doing manual work such as housework or teaching children in the homes of the community.

At the beginning of the thirteenth century, these women grouped their cabins into what was called a Beguinage, and appointed one of their group as a mistress. Unlike those who entered monasteries, they did not renounce ownership of property. In time, as their number increased and they spread into southern France, they often lived in a common house and had a common purse.

During the Middle Ages, women had few legal rights. Throughout Europe the law attempted to preserve property in the family, and for children. Thus a widow, whether with children or without, was usually entitled only to the interest or profit from the property while she lived.

The development of guilds, brotherhoods of trades, during the Middle Ages, helped in the protection of widows. Each guild helped its own needy members and cared for their widows and orphans. Women were admitted to guilds if their husbands had been members. In this respect, however, a widow was limited in what she could do with her husband's business upon his death. One guild law stated that if any woman who was the wife of the maker of coral or shell rosary beads married a second husband who was not of the craft, she could continue in the craft but not take on apprentices. A glasscutters and gemworkers guild also ruled that no master's widow who kept working at this craft after her husband's death could take on apprentices. A woman was considered unable to teach a child to master such a delicate craft.

The idea of asceticism, including chastity, was promoted by monasteries during this period. Virgins, widows, and even wives could leave their homes and move into the cloisters to become "brides of Christ." Even at home with her husband, a wife was exhorted to practice chastity. She was taught that Joseph and Mary lived celibate lives, and though her husband might be forgiven the minor sin of begetting a child or so, the sooner the couple achieved the ideal of married chastity, the better for both of them. Married chastity, it was said, would bring forth spiritual fruit thirtyfold; widowed chastity, sixtyfold; and virginal chastity, one hundredfold. A consecrated nun received even higher rewards.

With the coming of the Reformation, priestly celibacy was renounced by the Protestant clergy. Many monks and nuns left monasteries to marry, and as a result some were closed and the lands taken over by the state. The monasteries had been the only place where women had been given official recognition by the church, so their dissolution is seen by some scholars as a setback for women. Women now had less opportunity to follow a religious calling, and young girls were denied the opportunity of education. Standards of education for women dropped during the fourteenth and fifteenth centuries.

The Reformation began with one of the most important marriages in history, when Martin Luther took to wife the former nun Katherine von Bora. Page Smith in *Daughters of the Promised Land* writes that their marriage stated in effect that the most fruitful life was not lived in the seclusion of a monastery or convent but in the world with all its conflicts and complexities. For several centuries, the father's function had been only to perpetuate his name and estate through a male heir. With new emphasis on family life, fathers took direct responsibility for the education of their daughters. Obviously, this helped to take away the reproach of the widow who had produced no sons to immortalize the father. The education women now received helped them to earn their own livelihood should their husbands die.

Neither Luther nor Calvin seems to have set an example of making women feel needed and wanted in the new Protestant faith. Elsie Thomas Culver says that the leaders of the Protestant Reformation ignored the fact that women were of tremendous value to the church, and failed to provide for them any challenging avenue of religious study and service in the new structures of Protestantism.

POST-REFORMATION TIMES

To trace the status of widows as a group becomes extremely difficult after this point. Because of extreme poverty during the early modern period, many people were poorly fed. Husbands sometimes deserted their families, abandoning the struggle to provide for them. The poverty-stricken mother who pleads for help is a recurrent figure in nineteenth century literature. Widows were plentiful and orphans more abundant, which led to development of orphanages, poor farms, poor laws, debtors' prisons. The widow had once again sunk to the bottom of society.

In Puritan America, however, a woman was worth a great deal because she was so essential to the economy. A farmer without a wife was severely handicapped. Because wives and mothers were in short supply, their value increased accordingly. "Poor females of scanty means" were encouraged to come to America if they were virtuous and sensible. Spinsters were rare, for most women were married before twenty-two, often before sixteen.

In America, women became butchers, silversmiths, gunsmiths, upholsterers, jailkeepers, printers, apothecaries, and doctors. When they were widowed, which happened often in those precarious times, they continued to run the farm, store, mill, tanning shop, inn, or newspaper. Sometimes they even took over control of a ship because no extra men were around. Eleven women ran printing presses and ten of these published newspapers in America before 1776. Colonial and frontier courts, recognizing these realities, stretched the common law to protect widows and single women.

A notice in a New York paper in 1733 read: "We, widows of this city, have had a meeting as our case is something deplorable, we beg you will give it place in your Weekly Journal, that we may be relieved, it is as follows. We are house keepers, pay our taxes, carry on trade and most of us are she merchants, and as we in some measure contribute to the support of the government, we ought to be entitled to some of the sweets of it."

On occasion young men married widows in their sixties, seventies, and even eighties, which shows the extent to which practical considerations rather than romance controlled such relationships during the early days of America. Governor Nicholson of Virginia believed that fewer men of ability were coming from England to America at the time because most of the lands had been taken up and the natives were marrying widows or maids with property.

The story of the Widow Storey is told in *Women of the Century*. When her husband was killed by a falling tree, she went from Connecticut to Salisbury, Vermont, with her ten children, to take his place preserving and clearing his farm. In spite of extreme hardship and danger, acre after acre of dense forest melted away before her axe. She piled the logs and bushes and burned them. She raised crops. She fished and hunted to support herself and her family. To protect herself from the Indians she dug an underground room with a small entrance under an overhanging thicket in the bank of the stream where she slept each night with her family. She worked in this manner alone until her sons could help her, eventually becoming an independent landowner.

TWENTIETH CENTURY

Widows today have inherited an image of poverty and uselessness from our unfortunate predecessors. In a society becoming increasingly concerned with sexual relationships, to this image has been added a third element: the widow is one left over after pairs have been made. Gains made during the time of Christ and the early apostolic church have been lost.

During the first part of the twentieth century, widows appear in books of etiquette with rigid restrictions on their outward behavior. Emily Post (1942) stated that the widow should wear a black dress with all trimmings removed to declare her devotion to her bereaved husband. She indicated it was sometimes customary to give away all colorful clothing, and even to dye dresses and suits and blacken shoes, during the period of mourning. The type of material a widow could wear was also restricted. She could choose from cotton, linen, wool, lusterless silks, uncut velvet, or crepe, but should abstain from cut velvet, lace, or satin. She should avoid fancy weaves in stockings and patent or satin shoes. She should wear little or no jewelry.

The widow's activities were also limited during mourning, which might last a year for a young widow, with an additional six months sometimes added and referred to as second mourning. An older widow might wear mourning for life or deep mourning for one year followed by a year of second mourning. She was not to appear in public or in restaurants or entertainments, except for the opera, concert, or theater. She was not to indulge in anything that might indicate "taking part in social gaiety"—no balls, dances, parties, groups. She was not to convey the impression of being ultrafashionable, boisterous, or flippant. Some widows wore small crepe bonnets with a short front veil and a long back veil reaching to the bottom edge of the skirt. After three months of mourning, the front veil was thrown back, but the long veil was sometimes worn for life.

These signs of mourning were adopted to honor the dead and to protect the family from undue frivolity. Everyone was to be aware that a death had taken place in the family and to show proper respect. Severe mourning made it difficult for widows to move back into society, forcing them into a decided "widow" role, which may have had some securities of its own. At the present time, a great show of mourning is considered old-fashioned. No outward signs now identify the widow to society, although she may wear her wedding band on her right hand or leave it off altogether.

In some earlier societies the widow was killed by strangling or burning in order to accompany her husband on his journey into the next world. Modern society performs its own strangulation by the social pressures it creates, forcing the uncoupled woman to wait out her life puttering in her garden, visiting, working at some job, always waiting, sometimes wishing her life had ended when her husband's did. What she needs is not more books on etiquette but someone to help her with her "grief work" and then when that has been done, to help her forge ahead once again with the business of living—to move beyond widowhood.

See page 303 for Bibliography.

CHAPTER FIFTEEN
Beyond Widowhood

Faith is the foot by which we go to Jesus. A lame foot is still a foot. He who comes slowly, nevertheless comes. —George Müller

A friend of mine was hospitalized for back surgery. Her operation had been more complicated, the resulting pain more severe, and the time spent in convalescence longer than anticipated. When I visited her, she commented wryly that the nurses had a standard response to all her complaints: "Take a deep breath."

I wasn't sure that deep breaths could relieve discomfort, but I went home from the hospital to experiment a bit. I found out you can't breathe deeply and think about the crossword puzzle you're doing. You can't breathe deeply and compose an article on the typewriter. Your mind is drawn to the effort of breathing. Deep breathing is a conscious act, not an unconscious one like the breathing we do in ordinary living.

Our regular-type breathing keeps us going when we're well. But when we lie flat in the hospital, with waves of nausea rolling over us and pain attacking slowly or violently, a nurse sometimes has to remind us to take a deep breath to take our mind off the pain.

God is like that. Take a deep breath, he says. Stop for a moment to steady yourself for the personal crisis of pain you're facing. Focus on Me, not on your loss of husband or your personal misery. Cast off anxiety and apprehension. I am here.

In my years as a widow I've found it easy to identify with a Charlie Brown cartoon tacked up on my bulletin board. Lucy asks Charlie what he thinks security is. He replies that it's sleeping in the back seat of the car when you're a little kid. "You've been somewhere with your Mom and Dad, and it's night, and you're riding home in the car, and you can sleep in the back seat. You don't have to worry about anything. Your Mom and Dad are in the front seat and they take care of everything." As a child, I often felt that wonderful feeling of security.

But, as Charlie reminds Lucy, suddenly it's over, and you never get to sleep in the back seat again. At some point in life that feeling of security slips away—at adolescence, perhaps later. For some women, that point is the moment she becomes a widow. The security of having another person in the home to share problems, joys, and decision-making is suddenly gone. She is alone. She sits in the front seat by herself and has to stay awake for everyone, including herself. The night clouds glower in the western sky. The road looks rutty and rough. What do I do now? she wonders.

Take a deep breath, says God. It will carry you through the immediate agony of the loss to new strengths, securities, and opportunities you never knew existed. You were a wife. Now you are a widow. Ahead lies a place for you, a secure one, as a person in the sight of God. But you must make that security yours by faith.

Each day in spring after the last snow has melted, I watch the tulips and crocuses I planted in fall push their way through the ground. Before the green tips greet the day, I wonder if I planted them too deep. Then one day they emerge strong and healthy, determined to establish their place in the sun. I rejoice.

Soon the robins return to nest in our elm trees. A meadowlark breaks the morning stillness with its cry of joy. Behind the house I hear the dove calling all nature to mourn with it. Before long the bustling sparrows will again set up housekeeping in the crosspiece of the clothesline pole, looking for a secure place for the summer.

Each year now as I watch summer gaining strength, I miss my children's annual attempts at "place-making." Tent-building was a regular summer activity as long as they were young. How many years has it been since James and Christine last hauled out blankets, tarps, curtains, and clothespins to create a tent of their own over the clothesline? Most of their energy was devoted to frantic pinning and stretching, very little to sitting in the stuffy compartment that resulted. But, sweaty and tired, they would finally eat crackers and Kool-Aid in "their own place."

I remember how as a young girl, I used to lie on the sunny side of the woodpile in our backyard, gazing into the blue sky with its free floating clouds, wondering about the place I would have some day.

Longing for an emotional niche where one can be free

to be oneself, to love, to risk failure, is almost instinctive. Many of us believe that when we find that place up ahead in life's journey where we'll fit in, it will be a good solid ledge—a stopping point where we can relax for a time. In other words, it will be an arriving. For some women, marriage is that ledge, that place of security, acceptance, identity, and happiness. For years a woman may enjoy the comfortable feeling of belonging, and then one day, like the tulips and sparrows, she must look for her "place" again.

We tend to forget that God never intended a Christian, married or single, to settle down and stagnate. Our place in God's economy is never a stopping point, like a better job, a bigger house, a more prestigious position. Our place always remains a journeying, a pilgrimage, as it was for Abraham and Moses. We must keep moving on to new challenges.

Widowhood challenges a woman to surrender her security in earthly things like finances, houses, possessions, even personal relationships. Rather she must trust more deeply in God and, through a leap of faith, move on. Each place in life, as she arrives at it, leads to another opportunity. Always the new place ahead involves risk and vulnerability. God gives security for awhile for her to gather courage to move on to new tasks.

A widow's grief and time of bereavement are only temporary stopping places. A widow cannot find her security in the role of husbandless woman, although she may be tempted to play the "professional widow" and find pride in it. Her calling is the continual pursuit of God. "I follow close behind you, protected by your strong right arm" (Psalm 63:8 TLB).

The children of Israel went through a difficult period during their exile in Babylon. Their life as a nation and as individuals had been disturbed to the roots. The prophet Isaiah viewed the seemingly hopeless situation of the exiled Israelites who remained true to God and comforted them: "Who is among you that feareth the Lord, that obeyeth the voice of his servant, that walketh in darkness, and hath no light? let him trust in the name of the Lord, and stay upon his God" (Isaiah 50:10). Isaiah was telling the righteous Israelite who couldn't see the way ahead to focus on God instead of on the pain of separation from his homeland.

I realize that faith is easily recommended as a remedy for spiritual darkness today. Faith is acceptable in a time of stress. The advice sometimes handed out to the troubled individual is simply to believe hard enough and everything will turn out all right. Christ himself said, "All things are possible to him that believeth." But he said more about faith than that. Teaching about the life of faith is interwoven in the whole Bible.

As Christians we certainly need faith, but faith in faith *per se* is emptiness. True faith believes the right things about the right person. A. W. Tozer says, "True faith requires that we believe everything God has said about Himself and also everything He has said about us." Such faith is overcoming faith. Isaiah said to the Israelite in darkness, "Trust in the name of the Lord." Trust in the Lord who is a shield, a fortress, a deliverer, as well as a light. Breathe deeply. He is with you.

During the early years of my widowhood I read much about the life of faith, for the answers I needed seemed to lie more in the spiritual realm than in greater financial

253

resources. When we stumble along in our spiritual lives, not knowing quite what we're searching for, sometimes a Scripture passage, a sentence in a sermon or a prayer, or a thought in a book suddenly articulates for us what we've been seeking.

Faith's Unclaimed Inheritance by Frank Houghton did that for me. The author divides humankind into two categories: Christian and non-Christian. Christians are again divided into two groupings. The larger group includes people who have "saving faith" for sins forgiven, but their faith stops short there. Their lives are hardly different from those of non-Christians. They have enough faith to save their souls but not enough to transform their lives. They're satisfied with life as it is, unaware of what Christian growth could do for them. The smaller group of Christians is aware that faith can change lives. Their desire is "How may I enjoy what God intends for a believer?" Though Hudson Taylor and George Müller are persons we admire and consider extraordinary Christians, they are the ones we should all be like. "Little-Faith" should be the exception, not the general condition of the Christian. The Christian life may be a battle, but it should end more often in victory than in defeat because God is on our side. And the victory is won by faith.

Yet what is faith? Not merely a beautiful feeling. Not the reward of works. Not some mysterious magic invoked through the right prayers. It is a conscious act of belief, a deliberate leaning of one's personality on God. It must become a habit of life. Just as we can develop a habit of worry and fear, we can develop a habit of trust, of leaning upon God's promises.

A little boy who had been taught that Jesus takes care of us in the dark was asked by his mother to get the mop from the dark outside porch. He hesitated to obey. The darkness frightened him.

"Jesus is with you," said his mother. "He will take care of you."

The little boy opened the door to the dark porch, thrust out his hand and said, "Dear Jesus, please hand me the mop."

He had faith to believe that Jesus was there, but not faith enough to trust his life to him. True faith is more than intellectual assent to the fact that God exists and that he is ready to answer. It involves complete commitment to him. At times it may mean going out onto the dark porch. Faith trusts God in darkness and in light, in sorrow and in joy, in marriage and singleness.

The prophet Isaiah had another word of encouragement for the Israelite in exile "who had no light." He was to "stay upon his God." The person in darkness was to wait upon God. The darkness didn't mean that God wasn't there. There was to be no frenzied activity, no feverish planning, but a resting, an expectation that he would reveal himself to the Israelites.

I sometimes think I've spent several lifetimes in expectant waiting: waiting for health to return, for children to grow up, for the opportunity to move into a vocation I enjoyed, for time to write, for children to come home for visits, for relief from work. Waiting can be voluntary or involuntary. It can be done deliberately with a sense of God's timing, or it can be done impatiently, brushing aside his plans in an urgent attempt to keep the action going. Waiting includes earnestness, quiet intelligent

seeking, faith that God keeps his word and never dis-
appoints. The revelation of God often comes after long
periods of waiting. We cannot manufacture rest or peace
for ourselves, but it comes only as we yield ourselves to
the working of his Spirit.

Waiting is difficult, more difficult than working or
planning or even praying. Waiting requires inner
strength. It requires submission to God's way whether
that way is darkness or light.

Yet waiting doesn't exclude the need for much prayer.
Time for prayer is hard to fit into today's hurried and
spectator-oriented life. When does one pray, if at all?
Before one goes to the ball game? After watching the
evening television program? Prayer and the late news or
a talk show don't always fit together well. Sometimes
prayer seems like an anachronism left over from several
decades ago, like hand-cranked cars or high-buttoned
shoes.

A woman wrote an article in a denominational journal
following the death of her son. With great enthusiasm
she informed readers that she had made "spirit" contacts
with her son through the instrument of a medium, and
that these contacts had given her proof of the resurrection of Christ. Readers responded with strong support for her testimony.

So intense is the desire to experience God that some
persons will interpret anything that arouses their emotions as being communication with God. Plain, old-
fashioned prayer doesn't work fast enough for those who
are anxious for experience. Some get turned off by the
neat little thoughts in devotional books, which admittedly are often little more than exercises in wit and allit-

eration. For others, prayer doesn't fulfill what they've been taught about it. So after keeping up the forms for awhile, as they get more involved in time-consuming activities, disillusionment causes them to drop prayer from their lives.

The apostle Paul wrote to young Timothy, "Now she that is a widow indeed, and desolate, trusteth in God, and continueth in supplications and prayers night and day" (5:5). One of the greatest challenges of a new widow's life is to learn what it means to pray in the Spirit. I found myself barnacled by concepts about this person-to-God communication system which weren't readily loosened.

For example, is prayer only for the weak Christian whose back is to the wall? If not, why do we rarely hear the healthy person, the wealthy person, the profession-ally successful person say "Pray for me." Is it the mark of strength or of weakness to ask another Christian to pray for us? Is prayer something a person can discard as he or she becomes more self-sufficient and independent?

Even harder for me to get rid of has been the idea that prayer releases the Christian from personal responsibil-ity and decision-making. In the ancient Greek theater when one of the mortal characters got into a particularly tight spot, a god appeared abruptly to help him out of his dilemma. The god was lowered to the stage from a machine or stage structure and was known as a *deus ex machina*, or literally, a god out of the machine.

In the early years of my widowhood I read and claimed for myself the many wonderful promises that God gave mothers without husbands to help guide the family to maturity. I claimed these promises as my right. At times I demanded that God hold onto his end of the agreement.

I felt certain that the years of my widowhood would be smooth sailing, free of problems, and that every little prayer I brought before him would be granted at the turn of a page.

Who hasn't at some time prayed for a *deus ex machina* who can be pressed into service with the push of a button or the lowering of ropes? Who hasn't prayed for wisdom and guidance about some difficult decision, and then waited in impatient agony for God to step down from his heavenly throne and wave a big STOP or GO sign like a flagman on the highway, forcing us to take the new way?

Who hasn't at times unconsciously wanted God to turn her into a puppet to spare her the painful process of deciding the next step or of advising a troubled teenager? Why don't we believe that true prayer arouses the believer to accountability as well as making God's grace available? The decision is always ours to make, even after God has showed the way. He never pushes us into the way, but as we take the first step he gives the strength to move ahead.

As you take that deep breath of trust, thank God for the puzzle of life that widowhood presents. Sometimes life is a crossword, jigsaw, and wire puzzle all tangled together. How did the apostle Paul expect the Thessalonians to thank God for *everything* in the rigamarole of life: sudden change, inflation, war, hunger, death of a spouse, sickness, difficult neighbors, busy life? How could he expect us today to thank God for the world's inequalities and injustices: racial prejudice, mental retardation, social deprivation of older people? How are people in underprivileged countries expected to thank God for their hunger, knowing that many Americans throw out five pounds of solid garbage per day and eat meat several times daily? How is the refugee of wars and revolutions to thank God for his multitudinous needs, for his lack of food, clothing, privacy for his family, and a sense of identity? How is a mother to thank God for the opportunity to raise her children alone?

The apostle Paul was aware of the problems facing humankind confronted with extreme suffering when he wrote the words, "In every thing give thanks: for this is the will of God . . . concerning you" (1 Thessalonians 5:18). He knew that people tend to blame God when circumstances go wrong. At such times they demand that God step in, or at least explain to them the reasons for lack of justice, for famine, war, illness, death. And if the answers don't satisfy them, their relationship with God slowly disintegrates. I don't condemn such individuals, for I've felt the same way at times. However Ann Landers may try to give her readers reasons for the problems of life, God never promised his people explanations for everything. Christ promised to be the Way, not the solution.

The apostle Paul wrote to the Romans that "all things work together for good to them that love God" (8:28). For some people this verse becomes the easy way out of difficult circumstances. When life is hard and answers scarce, for such people the simplest approach is to claim squatter's rights and say in resignation, "It's the Lord's will." Whatever happens is their lot in life and eventually things will work themselves out without their lifting a finger.

There is another way of looking at "all things." When they are unanswered questions of death, sickness, in-

259

justice, and prejudice, they must become a challenge to the Christian. These tensions must be accepted deliberately and aggressively and given opportunity to work themselves out creatively in the individual's life. This can happen only if the individual sees such trials, not as circumstances which God has deliberately engineered to torment, but which in his omniscience he has permitted to happen. With such an attitude we are free of conflict with people who frustrate or hinder us. We are free to thank God that he is with us in the experience of bereavement, whatever trial it brings, and in the period of readjustment.

Faith is willingness to trust God when the pieces don't fit, as well as willingness to trust when life again moves along smoothly, as it will. It's not so important for a widow to know why God permitted the suffering as it is for her to accept the tension and anguish it has created in her life, and transform it. The valley of Baca must become a well. Rain must fill the empty pools. Suffering must become creative.

Late one evening I checked out ten or twelve books at the university library where I was enrolled in some courses. I finished at the main desk and then moved to the exit where a student makes a final check to make sure no book leaves the building without being properly stamped. As the young man at the door saw my heavy armload of books, he groaned audibly. He would have to open ten books to see if each one had a date. One or two books at a time were all right, but ten—that was too much.

Most of us dread the monotony of repetitive action. We resent and resist a steady routine of any kind because it kills the emotions. We don't like motion without meaning or progress. The single life can sometimes appear to be like that. Yet some widows who fear the boredom of life alone also fear the challenge of creative activity, of rising above mere existence to a level where they're expected to bring something new to life out of the storehouse of their resources. Creativity is a scary burden they'd rather not pick up.

A record my children found enjoyable was Simon and Garfunkel's "El Condor Pasa":

> I'd rather be a sparrow than a snail
> I'd rather be a hammer than a nail
> A man gets tied up to the ground,
> He gives the world its saddest sound.

The yearning to be a sparrow, flying in the open skies, exists in most people living alone. But because they fear the heights without a husband's strong arm to guide them, they choose the monotony of a snail's life. They would rather grub and burrow in the ground than live the free life on wings. And then they give the world its saddest sound: "Widowhood is hell on earth."

In every age there are persons who cling to the ground, who hug the mediocre, the sordid, the gross, the sinful. They like being snails, because they've never known that life on wings is possible. John Milton wrote about people who "walk in their dungeon in the mid-day sun." Wordsworth said they "have given their lives away, a sordid boon." Even the apostle Paul wrote about himself as one who had been bound but now was free.

To move beyond widowhood the Christian woman should seriously consider creativity as a way of life, for creativity and Christianity are closely linked. Unfortunately for the church, creativity has frequently been left to unbelievers as their domain. Christians have a right to claim creativity as our heritage, for when we create something new out of existing materials we are engaging in Godlike activity. Our new creation, whatever it may be, has a life of its own when it leaves the hand of its creator, as man and woman received life from God's hand. What a person creates cannot be created again. It is his or hers alone to give to others. No person can take it away.

The widow who chooses creativity as a way of moving beyond the bonds of misery and sorrow will need an active imagination. Imagination is another word almost totally rejected from some Christians' vocabulary because the connotations have come to mean unreal, made up, fictional, even deceitful. Imagination has come to mean something that doesn't really exist, an empty vision.

Yet a sanctified imagination is basically the faith of the soul, a way of seeing life under the guidance of the Spirit. The apostle Paul referred to it as "having the eyes of your hearts enlightened" (Ephesians 1:18 RSV). It takes creative imagination to see beyond the shriveled soul in its snail armor, dragging itself along in worn-out patterns to the glory that can exist when the grace of God enters its life.

An old Tibetan proverb says, "The only sin is to live in worn-out patterns," to let oneself be chained to a pattern of life that is empty and meaningless. The biggest crime a widow commits against herself is never to see beyond the ordinary, never to look higher than a snail's level simply because she is a widow. A creative Christian is ready to move away from familiar patterns of life, if need be, even though she may begin with something very common and ordinary in her effort to bring beauty to her life and to others.

An unimaginative person, given a task, will choose the easiest, most familiar, and least taxing path. I see this tendency in some of my students. What's the quickest way I can get this assignment done? they ask. The imaginative person looks for a way to strike out and express individuality. Such a person doesn't want to stay in ruts. The unimaginative person looks for ruts because they spell security.

I see the Pharisees as unimaginative persons. They supported the old ways of doing things, though these old patterns kept people stuck to the ground. They heard people all around them uttering sad sounds, yet they demanded that the Jews stick to the old patterns because the law demanded they do so. They lacked the imagination to see the spirit of the law. Their philosophy of life blinded them to seeing life as more than dotting i's and crossing t's. They didn't see the man in pain, knocked down by robbers. They clung to worn-out patterns because they were afraid of the insecurity of creative living, where there were no exact boundaries.

Then Christ came and said, "There's another way. You don't have to be a snail dragging yourself along the ground. It's possible to fly." But the Pharisees didn't understand. They couldn't stretch their spirits to match his, so they tried to stop him with a cross.

Some widows have been pushed into sorrow, loneliness, and misery. They think they have to stay there because society has created a role for them. They don't recognize Christ's call to a life on wings.

Christ showed his creative approach when he chose Peter—impulsive, unschooled, inarticulate Peter. A creative imagination enables one to see beyond the pragmatic and the present to another dimension. It enables the individual to see the whole when one has only a small part as yet. For example, a potter who holds a lump of clay in his hands can see the finished bowl in his mind. Similarly, a composer can hear his composition before it has been performed. He knows what it sounds like. Christ saw what kind of person Peter would be when the Spirit controlled his life.

Christ saw in Mary Magdalene, out of whom seven devils were cast, a person who would bring glory to God when she was redeemed, instead of dragging herself and others into degradation.

Christ saw in Zacchaeus, the Scrooge of Bible times, a man who was lonely and alone. He saw the part that foreshadowed the whole redeemed life and began to work with that part.

But the Pharisees couldn't understand what it was all about. Like some surface-living people today who refuse to let their imaginations work, they mutter, "There goes a man who doesn't love God." A creative imagination says, "There goes a man whom God loves. There goes a person who may be mad at his parents, mad at life, mad at God, who seems intent on wrecking his life, yet one whom God considers worth redeeming."

I believe that loving and caring begin in the creative imagination of the Christian. Empathy is the ability to identify imaginatively with another's cares and burdens

---

and feel them as if they were our own. The Pharisaical approach was "an eye for an eye and a tooth for a tooth," *i.e.,* the exact fulfillment of the law. Christ said, "Be creative. If a person asks you to go one mile, go two miles with him. If he asks you for your coat, give your cloak also. If he hits you on one cheek, turn the other." Creative imagination gives a widow the opportunity to become an instrument of reconciliation to those who live in conflict, fear, sorrow, hate, and want.

This approach has wide ramifications. It makes it possible to turn the bitter experiences of life into something new and glorious by the grace of God. The widow who develops this enlightenment finds life opening up in many other ways. The smallest details of life lose their humdrum quality. A talkative neighbor is more than idle chatter, but an opportunity to discover God in that relationship. Living alone becomes an opportunity to share time with other lonely people or to develop new skills. Failure is no longer a threat to new experiences. A widow can risk looking back at the past, acknowledge the good, turn to the future, and trust that love and faith will be there also.

In addition to imagination, the widow who chooses the way of creativity will find she needs discipline. A creative work, whether a poem, a piece of sculpture, a novel, or a new friendship, doesn't take shape by itself. The artist has a plan before he begins. Orville and Wilbur Wright had a vision of man in flight. This vision pursued them and they pursued it until it became a reality.

A creative Christian needs to know God's purpose in her life, so she can speak of it to others: "I have a vision that the grace of God can work in X's life. I have a vision

265

of human beings in this community living in peace. I have a vision that will result in closer fellowship for the elderly." Our success or failure won't depend on how well educated we are, how much money we have inherited, but on our trust in God's purposes for our life. Call it a sense of destiny, if you will. When we know this, we have security, a safe place all our own, and we are secure enough to reach out to others.

Finally, a creative widow will also need courage. We can't be creative with fear as our keeper. Fear demands too much. I know. Every time I sit down to write, I struggle with the fear of what people will think about what I've written. Fear knows how to use my typewriter, often better than I do. "Play it safe," he says. "Use the party line. Don't rock the boat. Make this sentence a little more general, less specific . . ." When fear is finished, I'm left with a mess of words resembling wallpaper paste. The creative life, creativity in almost any area of life, is always an adventure of faith. It requires willingness to deal with truth in our relationships with God and humankind—and willingness to risk failure and criticism.

The words of Hannah Whitall Smith have encouraged many people who have suffered. She illustrates the difference in the ways three women might face a spiritual mountain. The first one would "tunnel through it with hard wearisome labor; the second would meander around it in indefinite fashion; but the third would just flap her wings and fly right over."

The problem is to learn to fly when we are still shrouded in our widow's weeds. Wings and feathers don't sprout easily from black mourning garments.

Some women facing widowhood adopt the method of the first woman. By dogged determination and hard work they plow their way through any obstacle before them: loneliness, boredom, gossip, discouragement, lack of satisfaction in Bible reading and prayer, illness, financial stress. I admit to having tried it, and it can be a hard, bitter course. Human strength is frail, and sheer determination a cruel taskmaster.

Choosing the way of least resistance by meandering around the obstacles or hoping they'll go away if we leave them alone looks like the easiest way. It never forces the individual to make a deliberate decision or decide on any issue. Mrs. Smith should have included another group of women in her illustration: those who, when they confront a problem or a decision, simply turn around and run. Jonah once found the situation he was in too tough, the assignment God had given him too difficult, so he turned tail and ran. Modern-day living has few whales to swallow us nor can most of us take off for the South Seas to bask in the sun while the world works out its problems. But it's possible to run away by swallowing instead of being swallowed—pills, alcohol, food. It's possible to avoid the mountains created by circumstances beyond our control, such as illness, death, financial difficulty—or the mountains we've created by worry and fear, by turning to work, shopping, talking, watching television, sheer activity, or simply griping.

Alvin N. Rogness tells a story which took place many years ago. A large American eagle was held in captivity in a frontier store, fastened by one of its feet to a chain secured by a ring in the floor. A young mountaineer saw the bird and purchased it from the store owner for two dollars. He took it to the outskirts of the village and before an interested crowd undid the chain. The great bird, however, remained motionless, and those who watched were disappointed. It had been so long bound to earth that it didn't care to fly. But then it raised its head to the sun and seemed to remember that it was an eagle with a home among the crags and cliffs. With a shriek it flew off.

The young man said, "I used to see that bird high up in the mountains while I was tending sheep and when I saw it chained in that store I couldn't stand it. It belongs up above and was never meant for a place like this."

I think this was what Hannah Smith intended to say when she urged us to take wing and fly over the obstacles. God never intended any of his children to grovel in the lowlands of despair, to be defeated by circumstances, to be held back by mountains of fear and worry. He intended those who call themselves his followers to be overcomers—literally, those who come over the mountains. Wings are given to those of his children who "wait upon the Lord . . . [for] they shall mount up with wings as eagles" (Isaiah 40:31). They shall fly. Beyond widowhood lies a life on wings.

Epilogue

CHAPTER SIXTEEN
Lost and Found

If you are willing to choose the seeming darkness instead of the illumination of reason, wonderful light will break out upon you from the Word of God. —A. J. Gordon

When I was a child, I seemed to have a knack for getting lost. Since then, I've been lost often, in many ways.

Once, when I was about ten or eleven, I became separated from my friends while visiting in a strange city. I trudged block after block trying to find my way back to my aunt's and uncle's house. I had one landmark: a large flour mill that loomed tall on the horizon miles from where I stood. I knew it was close to my relatives' home. I headed in that general direction. On either side of the street, as I walked, house after house squatted smugly, taunting me in my lostness. My legs grew wearier, my spirit more dejected with each step. I wanted to crawl into the cracks in the sidewalk with the grasshoppers. The flour mill never got closer. I was conquered by the bleak realization that no amount of cheerfulness or courage could help me find the way back. I was lost. Finally, a kindly policeman noticed my dilemma and redirected me. I could go home again.

Another time, while swimming with some cousins in an indoor salt-water swimming pool, I managed to make my way to a center island with the coaxing of friends. But they returned to the shallow end without me. I couldn't swim, and walking was out of the question. The water was beyond my depth. I knew I was drowning, but I hadn't done enough swimming to know that all I had to do was holler for help. As I floundered in the water, the salty brine taste cut the back of my throat and nose and pained my eyes. I reached and reached for the handrails. My toes stretched to touch bottom but found no footing. It was bottomless. Gasping, weary, and humiliated, I finally made it to safety. I never told anyone about the experience.

But my lostness hasn't always been geographical or physical. It has also been spiritual, emotional, and psychological. Each time, I experienced anew the same awful feeling I'd had in the pool, sinking endlessly and not finding the bottom, rising only to go down again.

I had grown up in a particularly free community. Our little village in northern Saskatchewan was composed of every nationality and every creed: Russian, Doukhobor, English, Scottish, Irish, French, Ukrainian, Indian, Polish, German. They were all there as well as some I have forgotten.

Our community was not particularly religious, but a few churches stood as sentinels at the corners of the town, keeping evil at bay—a Roman Catholic church with a fairly large parish and a 7:30 A.M. bell calling its parishioners to mass; a United Church of Canada with a

good-sized Sunday school, a dwindling Ladies Aid and a
meager attendance at other services; an Anglican church
in which a visiting minister held services once a month; a
Russian Baptist Church with exuberant singing. Christianity was important in my family. Since churchgoing was
needed for respectable living, and since our own denomination wasn't represented in the community, we
lived a double life. In summer we were Mennonite
Brethren; in winter, Mother and Dad were Russian Baptist and we children, who couldn't understand Russian,
were United Church. It seemed like a fairly satisfactory
arrangement for all.

My storekeeper father's ambitious goal for his four
daughters and one son was to give us each sufficient
education to make us self-supporting, independent persons. As a new immigrant to this country, who had been
unable to receive an education in the Mennonite colonies
of the Ukraine in Russia, he valued education highly as
the steppingstone away from manual labor to a freer life.
My mother supported him in his goals for us. Marriage
was expected in a vague sense, but the passive homemaker role wasn't vocally stressed. As I rethink this early
part of my life, I remember clearly how Dad admired
women in the community who were decisive contributors
rather than empty bits of feminine fluff. He evoked in us
a pride in being a person: "You are a Funk." None of us
ever forgot that. Contact with our own church twenty
miles away across the Saskatchewan River, was seasonal
and spasmodic because of weather and road conditions
(no cars traveled in winter and we had no horse and
sleigh), but our upbringing was clearly Christian. Dad, a
person who had never wholly supported any kind of

hierarchical church structure, served God faithfully in his own personal life, even doing extensive preaching and evangelistic work in his early years. He paid distant homage to the institution. I think we children enjoyed our ecclesiastical freedom.

By a strange set of circumstances I found myself living in a convalescent home shortly after I left high school to work in the city. Perhaps living so close to people who had lost their firm grip on life caused me to think seriously that summer. Life was busy, but it was dull; I had a job, but I couldn't call it a vocation. I called myself a Christian, but I wasn't a disciple. Even reading had palled, though I carried home loads of books from the library, hoping to find something to fill the void in my heart. But the words were all empty, dispersing like chaff before the wind.

One Saturday morning I was bookless. Like a caged animal I wandered about, searching for something to do. Finally, in the sunroom, as I rummaged through some untidy shelves of old books and papers, I came upon a grubby looking book. As I carelessly leafed through it, I noticed it was a religious book. Any book was better than no book, so I took it to my room.

The book turned out to be a volume of daily devotional readings. So, much as I had often sought a penny fortune in a slot machine, I turned to September 1 to read what had been written for that day. The words of Scripture leaped from the page: " 'Ye shall be holy; for I am holy' (1 Peter 1:16 RV). Continually restate to yourself what the purpose of your life is. The destined end of man is not happiness nor health, but holiness."

To find the right words for the right moment is an

emotional experience akin to discovering a gold mine. I stared at the words as ideas tore loose and raced in all directions within me. This book I clutched in my hand was telling me what I wanted to know. I read quickly, eagerly, to the end of the page.

That day, my weak faltering faith received strength. My aimless feet were put on course. My ambitionless life was given a goal. A lost sheep was found. A rebellious spirit yielded to a Master.

Much as I would have liked to keep the book for myself, I returned it to the shelf in the sunroom after typing a copy of the reading for myself. I forgot, however, to write down the title of the book. Several years later a friend presented *My Utmost for His Highest*, by Oswald Chambers, to my husband and me as a wedding gift. When within a few weeks I came upon the familiar selection for September 1, I recognized the book I thought was lost to me forever. Since then I've dipped into all kinds of devotional books, but soon drop them to return to the timeless writings of Chambers.

Very soon after I found the book, I became an active member of the local youth group in the city where I was working, about sixty miles from home. We were the "Jesus people" of our time, during World War II, when "youth fellowships" of every nature and description blossomed across the country. The will of God for our lives, Christ's love for mankind, fellowship, and Bible study became our passion. I recall those years with fondness.

I read my Bible avidly to find out more about this exciting Christian way and in my newfound zeal spoke up openly in youth meetings. My eager tongue and ambitious plans for our youth group soon got me elected president, not totally a surprise, for I had enjoyed being part of the action in my high school where no one worried about such matters as sex discrimination. Within a matter of weeks, though, some of my "young brethren," at the request of the pastor and church council, asked me to resign. Something about my shape and bodily functions made it impossible for me to continue in the office. Because God's glory was more important to me than youth group presidencies, I readily consented. Perhaps I had misunderstood God's will.

Becoming youth president wasn't the last time I was to blunder unknowingly into off-bounds territory because I took seriously "Whatsoever thy hand findeth to do, do it with all thy might," forgetting to add, "only if the church allows women in this area."

Only much later did I seriously wonder that if the Lord's work is important and a woman is the person best suited for the task, why isn't she allowed to do the work? I have since noticed that a man with little experience and enthusiasm for a work will often be chosen when better prepared and more interested women are left on the sidelines as a cheering section. Why is it that women who carry much individual responsibility in the church are only rarely asked to help shape policy concerning that work?

After several years of working as a legal secretary and two years in college, I married, expecting to spend the rest of my life safely isolated from society, secure in my husband's love, caring for my children and home. I never saw myself in any other role and never suspected I might be forced to seek one. I never saw myself other than as a contented wife and mother. Never middle-aged. Never alone.

Married life began for Walter and me as it does for so many other newlyweds, as a big glorious adventure of togetherness. Together we would conquer life and serve our God. That heady feeling of "winner take all" soon fled before the burden of cramped quarters, limited budgets, and lonely days as a student's wife and later as a young pastor's wife.

We were faced with the added challenge of a low income, and the fact that my husband wanted to complete his education, interrupted by the war. I took a deep breath and dived in, intent on becoming the best Christian homemaker possible.

Very soon I sensed a certain frustration and bitterness creeping in. As a single person I had become extremely interested in all aspects of the work of church and denomination. Working for a while in a church college office as secretary, I had become familiar with all aspects of our programs. Now, all of that except children's work in the local church, the sewing society, and musical activities were off limits. My intellectual life had dwindled pathetically, so I returned to studying the Scriptures and other books. But I could find nothing to answer my uneasiness about myself as a *person*. The church seemed to address me only as a woman (who should ask no questions), not as a person (who happened to be female).

Only later did I realize that my uneasiness was part of a syndrome affecting women all over the nation—women between thirty and forty who had probably dropped out of school to marry, moved to the suburbs, had children; whose husbands moved into business or professions; and who one day found they had stopped growing in order to satisfy that one goal in life—to marry and have children. I was caught in the current of the rapid changes taking place regarding a woman's role in life. Betty Friedan, who wrote *The Feminine Mystique*, didn't cause it; she merely drew attention to it. Questions I'd been asking for years now demanded answers. Once again I was a lost pilgrim.

I found myself asking questions such as "Who really am I? Am I a person first or a woman first? Do I have to think of myself only in terms of the roles in life I have to fill, such as wife and mother, much as I enjoy them?" In our small preacher-conscious church world, husbands were status symbols, and some women received their sense of importance and identity through the prominence of their preacher-husbands in church and conference work. Even my naive mind soon sensed that such an approach was a strange way of getting relevance out of life, for it resulted in great concern for a husband's offices and positions and much criticism of his sermons and programs.

Could I find sufficient meaning in life being the wife of the Rev. Walter Wiebe, a young minister, without making any specific contribution to life on my own? Must I live my life through him and the lives of my children? To do so wasn't unusual. My mother had had no other ambition in life. What would happen if Walter died? Who would I be then? What would give meaning to my life as a widow? What made the agony even more intense was that I felt guilty even questioning what seemed right and pure: that a woman should find complete fulfillment in her role as wife and mother and never expect God to require anything more of her. She had found her sphere of service. I felt burdened with guilt at thinking I was failing God by questioning traditional interpretations of the Word of God. Was I sinning by wanting to serve God with gifts I thought I had in writing, for example? Was I actually only trying to wiggle out from under the authority of God's Word?

I had begun married life with the idea that it would be my whole life, so I kept myself busy at domestic tasks. I sewed all the children's clothes and my own, even coats at times. I gardened and canned up to 400 or more jars of fruit and vegetables each year. I learned a little about butchering. After psyching myself up with strong words of encouragement, I could even enter the henhouse, corner a young rooster, persuade him to lie still on the chopping block, and lop off his head, even though my heart pounded as wildly as his beheaded body once the head was gone.

I became an active church worker in Sunday school teaching, women's work, children's work. I still think with some joy about the girls' Bible club we conducted one winter in our pastorate. I helped my husband as his secretary. I enjoyed the creative challenge of many aspects of this work. I gave the church and my family everything I could, but I gave myself very little—because to listen to myself was to bring on feelings of guilt.

The harder I worked to fulfill the role of successful church woman, the more futile it seemed. I wanted desperately to serve God and do what the church taught regarding women. Yet there seemed to be an empty rhetoric here not substantiated by my own experience. I had some private conversations with a few women who, though they spoke publicly of being "happy in the Lord," were inwardly disquieted by the direction their lives were taking. I wondered why, if Christianity was an authentic option for women of the twentieth century, it didn't make them exciting, alive persons.

I became increasingly aware of the forces of society and church pushing my husband and myself in two different directions, so unlike our college experience when we'd had common interests. We had worked together on the school newspaper and in other activities, side by side. Now we were members of the same church in which he had first-class citizenship and I second-class. He went to the policy-making meetings; I attended women's meetings and mission rallies. He helped make decisions; I served coffee. He studied the Word of God; I sewed and hunted for bargains in clothing and tracked down recipes and telephoned.

When we visited friends, the interesting talk was usually in the men's corner, where they discussed doctrinal issues and church politics. We women had to content ourselves with hemline lengths, new knitting patterns, canning successes and failures. (We must have realized subconsciously that the agony and ecstasy of the Christian community would never really be ours.)

I plunged into women's work, and for a while found it satisfying, although the perennial questions about where women belong were annoying. Are women's groups an auxiliary to the main body of the church to serve and assist the men (the true church), or can they function as full-fledged organizations in their own right? It bothered me to see some women's organizations forming what was actually a little church and conference parallel to the main body. Both men and women seemed oblivious to what was happening because they believed that God's pattern for the church was a strong group of men moving the church along, and another group of women establishing their own hierarchy of presidents and treasurers, finding full satisfaction in their own pursuits (usually overseas missions). Neither group seemed free enough to say, "Let's work together."

It also saddened me when sometimes the extent of our women's fellowship was to encourage each other to hang a Scripture verse above the kitchen sink: "I can't do much else for the Lord, but as I wash my dishes I can think nice thoughts." To me, at the time, women seemed so easily satisfied with what seemed like the safe roles, yet were actually the most dangerous because they so easily led into lethargy.

In the typical women's group, I could see no potential Catherine Booth or Mary Slessor or Florence Nightingale. Was embroidering tea towels and quilting really what God wanted of most women in the church in this desperate age? Was there no legitimate purpose for education other than insurance against a husband's early death? What should a woman do with the longing within her to enjoy the craftsmanship of writing, painting, teaching, leading? I wondered. I agonized. Adding to the agony was the knowledge that women who find full satisfaction in cooking and cleaning can't understand their sister's dilemma. I was misunderstood.

I was looking for an identity that satisfied God's Word and fit the times in which we lived. I didn't know where I belonged, and this time it was harder to find help. No policeman was around to direct me. Even Oswald Chambers seemed to have nothing to say. Magazines were full of articles about the growing pains of women my age, but the church was strangely silent. When I talked to men about the matter, some were immediately threatened and defensive, very unready to yield position or make room for women in the church other than in traditional roles. If they did budge, it was frequently with an attitude of dispensing favors to the peons. Few women I spoke to at that time had the liberty to consider what seemed heresy. The Bible had sufficient texts that I should know my role, they said. Answers had to come from elsewhere, not because I rejected the Bible but because the array of interpretations was more confusing than helpful.

Some of the first glimmers of light came from a combination of reading Scripture and other writings. I stumbled one day upon Christ's words, "Thou shalt love thy neighbor as thyself." I'd read these words hundreds of times, probably, but suddenly they took on new meaning. Love myself? Who had ever heard of such a thing? One was supposed to love others, but to love oneself? How did one do such a thing?

I think that in the church we have stressed too much that life is for dying. During my developing years I so often heard preaching about death to self: "He must increase, I must decrease." I went through young adulthood believing that it was scriptural to hate oneself, that it was important to die to self, to become a "nothing" so that Christ could become everything. "Self" and "life" became almost dirty words. A Christian had no right to think of self-actualization.

I watched Christians struggling toward the goal of becoming "channels only," "instruments," and also "meek, insignificant worms" like Jacob. People prayed for an opportunity to serve God "in all weakness."

It is true that Scripture teaches death to sin and the carnal self, but it also teaches being alive to God. As I studied the Bible, particularly newer translations, I found that Christ said many things about self and the quality of a person's life on this earth (Matthew 16:24-28 NEB). Paul assured the Ephesians that life has purpose (Ephesians 5:15 Phillips). Christ talked about wholeness of personality and a full life. I began to doubt that a wormlike creature has a very significant or meaningful life. Christ intended his followers to make life itself their vocation while on earth and to use all the gifts he had given them in creative self-expression.

Any object, or life itself, becomes meaningful if it's worth something to someone. A Christian's life is worth a great deal to God. Didn't God love the world so much that he gave his Son for it? If he loves individuals that much, we have reason to love ourselves—at least as much as we love our neighbor. When we give our lives over to God, God gives us back our true selves to serve him. We become stewards of our personality. God doesn't return to us a shell or an empty husk of a body with the Holy Spirit rattling around inside. He gives each believer an individual personality, gifts, and talents sanctified by the Spirit.

Christ living in me—not in a worm—that was meaningful living. I had to learn to accept myself as God had made me and accepted me: race, sex, height, size; outgoing yet timid, ready to explore any new idea yet sometimes overzealous, energetic, dependable, demanding too much of others as well as of myself. I had to accept myself first of all as a person, not a woman. Mary at the feet of Jesus saw herself as a person, not as a woman whose role it was to serve the men a meal. Priscilla, Phoebe, and Dorcas seemed to do likewise. Maybe there was room for me in that group. Yet I knew that without present-day role models and supporting organizational structures in our conservative church organization, the way wouldn't be easy to fit into a nontraditional role. And it wasn't.

I cherish the words of Dr. Marion Hilliard, a medical doctor, who before her early death did considerable writing about women's role and problems. The world needs women to be persons, she said, rather than females playing various roles upon demand. "From the time a woman is born until she dies, she is not only a woman, but also a person." Unless she regards herself in this way, she will be "whatever the economy asks, or what the men think beautiful, or what the children want to make them happy . . . She is a person above all."

Bonhoeffer wrote that God doesn't ask a man to come to him to crush his identity and will. Yet to accept the traditional mold for women seemed to crush my own personhood. I simply wasn't prepared to spend my life embroidering as a way of serving God. I did such things as a hobby. I needed to accept myself as I was, even though others might consider me strange if I chose reading over canning and writing over quilting.

To accept myself meant accepting some of my secret urges and longings. As a high school student I had softly penciled to myself in a journal my desire to be a writer. In Jesus' parable, the man who failed to develop his talent was condemned to "outer darkness." His sin was failing to reach God's mark for him. The woman who was caught in adultery was told to "Go and sin no more." What a difference in punishment.

Somehow we have the idea that God's will for us will always be disagreeable and will require the breaking of our will to accept. Are anguish and misery prerequisites to doing the Lord's will? I am thankful that the newer books on the gifts of the Spirit point out that God has no desire to crush our creativity. He wants to help us fulfill our potential, whether we are wives, mothers, widows, or single. Doing so need not destroy family solidarity.

When I committed myself to what I believed to be God's gift to me, and began writing, I felt like an old horny toad that has come out from under a dank log and joined the human race. My living space suddenly enlarged and I had room to grow. I could face the sun and show my praise about the joy of living in this direction.

My first step was to set up a small table with my typewriter on it under the chimney corner of our parsonage. It became "Mom's desk." I was doing something pleasant, exciting, and profitable to me. I wrote a few news releases for a church periodical. I got back words of praise. I was launched, but not yet sailing. I didn't expect other women to adopt my pattern of living, for I believe God leads each person individually. I hoped only that my friends and neighbors would allow me to develop my skill in writing as I allowed them to develop theirs in cooking and cleaning. Not all of them understood me, yet I have never regretted my decision. I could now do the cooking and dusting more joyously.

While doing some research in church history, I read about a young woman in Manitoba in the 1870s, who, as a young wife with a good-sized family, about five or six children, took a course in midwifery in a distant city at the suggestion of the church, and in the absence of a doctor in the area delivered over 700 babies during her lifetime. No harsh words were spoken against her because she gave her life to God as a "career" woman in addition to serving her family. Perhaps it was that kind of open encouragement from the church I longed for as I struggled with acknowledging my own gift. Yet I cannot blame the church, for, as fearfully as I, it too was moving through uncharted ground, in regard to women's increasing demands for more living space.

My early writing attempts led to helping my husband in his work of editing a small periodical for youth workers in the church. I enjoyed the creative activity, and, as my husband became more active in other church duties, the editing became mostly my effort. When he suggested to the administrative committee that because I was doing most of the work and apparently quite successfully, I be appointed editor, their reaction was negative. They couldn't engage a woman as editor. I was baffled. I thought of Florence Nightingale's words in 1850: "I offered the church my heart, my mind, and all my life, but it sent me to do crochet work in my grandmother's parlor."

Again I became aware that the church doesn't fully reckon with its women as a spiritual force other than in Sunday school work with children, in the home, or in the church kitchen. For an overseas missionary, strangely, doors open a little crack. But women missionaries had mentioned to me repeatedly that though they carried heavy work loads, they were shut out of the decision-making meetings that covered their field of work. Frequently they had to get their information indirectly from a male missionary's wife.

By this time it was clear to me that self-development lay partly in the direction of more systematic study, a step I was very glad I took before Walter's death. My children were fast growing up, so the year when Walter was studying in Syracuse, New York, and I was alone with the children, I worked out a fairly structured program of reading together with them. I believe that in our age when people are surfeited with football scores and stock market reports, but starved for vision, the reading of great literature is one of the best ways to restore a sense of one's responsibility to others as well as to God. To read is to know more clearly that all people travel the same path from birth to death, and that on this path what is required of each one, man or woman, is "to do justly, and to love mercy, and to walk humbly with thy God" (Micah 6:8).

A friend once remarked as he noticed what I consider my very modest library, "You have a lot of money stuck in books." Not stuck, but invested. The forest of life is sometimes dark and thick. Any book that opens a pathway through the underbrush is worth the investment.

For a time I wrote book reviews for a religious periodical when one of the regular reviewers couldn't keep up. I began writing a column for women in our denominational organ with the underlying assumption that my words might somehow help them live better lives as women of the home and church. Perhaps it was only a presumption. I knew that my column couldn't include the trivia so frequently encumbering a women's page and poured upon them by secular women's magazines. But the more troubling question was, why a "women's corner" at all in a church paper? Why not also a men's corner telling them to tack Scripture verses above their desks or to love their children and wives more? The great need in homes seems to be better fathers, fathers who are more aware of their responsibility to bring up children in a time when home influences are dwindling. Why did women need that kind of specialized treatment?

I struggled with the question for several years. The basic assumption seemed to be that women were very different creatures from men, perhaps not quite so human, requiring a different approach or a different interpretation of certain passages of Scripture. And one of the main ones seemed to be that they must be kept "in their place," whatever that meant. Their service was usually determined by limitations rather than freedom.

I took a major step in my pilgrimage the day I recognized I had to write as a person to persons, not just as a woman to women. If what I had to say was worthwhile, it couldn't be pushed into a corner just for women. I could see women only as an integral part of the whole church, not a secondary group who required separate treatment and were encouraged to keep flowers in the sanctuary and to send letters to missionaries. I decided to change the name of my column from "Women and the Church" to "Viewpoint," fearfully, and against some opposition. My mild sense of freedom wasn't obliterated completely by the knowledge that though *I* might regard myself as a person, many readers would still regard my words as coming from a woman. Sure enough, several years later, readers still approached me about the "women's column"

I was writing. But I found I did gain wider readership and a larger field of ideas to write about.

Writing has forced me to face the question of honesty. Every time I shared with others my vision in my writing—sometimes blurred by personal circumstances, other times a little clearer—I struggled with certain questions: How much should I write about the contradictions I see between theory and practice, and the way we in the church often pretend all is well? How generous can we afford to be in our praise of new trends? How much should we protect the image of the church as a successful progressive entity?

I found that to preserve my own integrity, I had to answer such questions, but not with catch-all phrases like "Let go and let God," or "The Lord will provide," or "Jesus is the answer." If I did, I would bow out of life as a contributing person.

As I continued to write, some readers sensed that my viewpoints changed on certain issues. That was inevitable as I continued to read and study and meet new experiences. I make no apologies for this. Change is necessary in an era of change. To change one's attitude can be a difficult and painful procedure because it means honestly facing what is inside one. To change means being willing to follow new light without guilt about what others will say. To change means being willing to admit that even God doesn't always hold one to his original instructions. To change doesn't necessarily mean one must reject the past. One can affirm the good in the past and move on to the new.

The experience of widowhood probably caused the greatest change in my thinking. I often thought of Abraham, the man whom God asked to sacrifice his son. Abraham was convinced that God wanted him to commit the act of killing the young man as a sacrifice. Yet at the critical moment, a ram appeared in the thicket and a voice told him to kill it instead of the boy. Abraham changed his actions to suit the change in instructions, yet hadn't God told Abraham to sacrifice his son? Maybe the voice was that of the devil in disguise and not an angel's?

Why didn't Abraham stick to his original convictions? Oswald Chambers says that Abraham, in his convictions about God, didn't make a fetish of being consistent.

As a widow, I had to accept this truth: Faithfulness to God is more important than faithfulness to tradition, or to earlier maps one has made for one's life.

I had accepted as my role in life, as the will of God, that I should be a housewife and mother. I never planned to leave that comfy spot. God had put me there. I liked my place. Then I was forced to change my role. Widowhood changed the road signs and sent me down a new path.

When my husband died, I thought I was lost again—but God has helped me find my way.

CHAPTER SEVENTEEN
by Christine Ruth Wiebe

The Year Daddy Died

In September 1962 our family lived in a miniature red brick house in Kitchener, Ontario. The house had two bedrooms. We were six people.

It never seemed small to me then. Because it was home, it was the right size. There I watched mother mix yellow food coloring with shiny white fat to make "butter"; our family ate *vreneke* (cottage cheese dumplings) for Saturday lunch after morning cleaning; and on Saturday afternoons I came in from play to smell both baking bread and Johnson's floor wax.

Life was simple and well ordered. Monday through Friday I attended third grade at a school that seemed several miles from home. I walked to school and back, stopping sometimes to watch a puddle with shiny rainbows floating on the surface. Mother didn't understand that my slow, thoughtful ways were the sign of a budding writer inside of me. She saw only that I was late getting home from school and gave me a spanking.

On Sundays our entire family went to church. While the grownups listened to a long German sermon, I went with the other children upstairs to an object lesson in English.

One Sunday we sang, "He lives, He lives. . . He lives within my heart." The lady at the front asked all those who knew that Jesus lived in their hearts to raise their hands. Most of the other children raised their hands, so I did too. I knew I didn't know Jesus, but I didn't worry about it.

All spare moments outside of church and school I spent either reading or playing with my best friend Donna who lived across the street. I was well fed, reasonably well clothed in hand-me-downs, and I had friends to play with. I didn't think about the future.

The future changed radically for me that fall in three separate events. The first occurred several weeks after school started. We moved from Kitchener to Hillsboro, Kansas. Daddy would have a job in a publishing house and we would live in a two-story house.

I was excited at the thought of traveling to a strange new place and living there, and about the house we would live in. We had a small photograph to look at while we waited for moving day. The house, white and sedate, hid behind great trees and bushes. It was a mansion after the boxlike structure we lived in then.

On the morning of our leaving, I watched my friend Donna walk down the sidewalk to school. Her wispy brown hair and reedy legs were already far down the street when I realized I would never see her again. A final goodbye was a new idea for me. Thoughts of what might happen to her and me floated in and out of my mind under the early morning sun.

"Goodbye!" I yelled after her. "We're leaving now!"

She didn't hear me. I watched as long as I could and finally went back in the house to take another load to the car.

When we were all ready, we climbed in our humble brown Chevrolet. The comfortable smell inside was dusty and old. From my corner in the back seat all I could see of Jamie, the baby, was his soft, cottony blonde hair. He was perched on a small suitcase between Mother and Daddy in the front seat.

We sat quietly in the driveway, the shadow of the small house sheltering us.

"Let's say the 121st Psalm," said Daddy.

Our voices joined in a chorus to say the words slowly, savoring each line.

> " I will lift up mine eyes unto the hills, from whence cometh my help. My help cometh from the Lord, which made heaven and earth. . ."

We always said this Psalm before going on a trip. The words made me feel jumpy and adventuresome because I knew they meant change. At the same time they made me feel safe and protected.

Daddy's deep voice prayed for several minutes. My mind wandered between the "Dear Father" and ". . . in Jesus' name we pray, Amen." Finally the car rolled slowly out of the driveway. We were on our way.

My first sight of our white "mansion" with its towering elm trees exceeded all expectations. On one side an overgrown lilac hedge divided our yard from the alley. Compared with the few spindly trees we had had in Kitchener, this was heaven. I knew I would be happy in Hillsboro.

A heavy rope swing dangled from one of the comfortable trees in the backyard. In the evening before it got dark, Daddy pushed me while I clung to the scratchy rope. Creak. Creak. The branch above me moved rhythmically, rustling the dry leaves.

We had a garage that was perfect for jumping off. With the neighbor children we explored the nearby railroad tracks, an abandoned house, and all the little buildings and sheds in the backyards of the old houses near us.

I followed Daddy around the yard as he raked leaves. Daddy was a tall, slender man with thin black hair. He didn't talk as he raked the leaves. He seemed to be thinking.

I was in third grade at the school at the other end of our street. The classes were much smaller than I was used to in Canada, and shockingly informal.

The first day in school the teacher, Mrs. Friday, asked me a question. In proper Canadian style, I stood up to give the answer. I heard some giggles in the back of the room, but I didn't understand what was funny. That evening Daddy was too tired to work outside. I sat quietly on his lap but I didn't tell him what had happened in school. His arm was around me. I felt warm and safe, as if I had drunk a cup of warm milk after an icy walk.

The second major event of the fall was less spectacular, but it has had more significant aftereffects than our move to Hillsboro.

One evening I had been thinking about death. As a seven-year-old, I wasn't afraid of death, but I was fascinated by the thought that at some point I would no longer exist. Finally I decided I needed help in my thinking.

"Daddy," I asked, "when do people die?"

He looked at me for some time and then, in his usual gentle way, he repeated my question. "When do people die, Chrissie?"

I don't remember all he said after that, but I remember we got on the subject of God, which often happens when one discusses death. And after death we talked about Jesus and being saved and what happens after death. The result was that he asked me if I wanted to ask Jesus into my heart.

"Why, yes," I answered. So I knelt beside a chair there in the living room with Mother and Daddy beside me. They each prayed for me and then I asked Jesus to come into my heart and forgive my sins. It was a simple, short prayer.

So I became a Christian that fall. At the time, my action seemed natural. I had done something I had intended to do since the lady in church had asked us to sing "He lives . . ." Only long afterward did I realize how significant a step I took that evening.

"When do people die?" I had asked my father. I had no idea my question would be answered so soon. The third event of the fall would answer it in a graphic way.

Toward the end of October, I spent more evenings on Daddy's lap and fewer evenings following him around the yard. Daddy was thinner and quieter. I didn't worry. He had been like that before and gotten better.

One night Daddy said gently, "I'm too tired tonight, Chrissie, for you to sit on my lap. How about getting a book and reading here beside me. I'm going to lie down and have a little nap."

The next night Daddy didn't eat supper. It was strange to have him lying on the couch in the living room and have Mother in charge at the supper table.

He was very sick, lying on the couch. I wasn't supposed to bother him. I walked past the door to the living room sometimes, to look in at him lying there.

I sat in a shadowy corner of the dining room, reading a book. I heard Mother and Daddy talking in low voices. After awhile Mother came back in the dining room and told me and my sisters she was going to take Daddy to the hospital. She went upstairs to pack a suitcase for him.

A heavy oak table stood in the middle of the dining room. It was sturdy and familiar. When Mother came back, she set the suitcase on the table. I didn't like it sitting there. The light overhead seemed to glare in my eyes and the table seemed cold and black.

Mother helped Daddy put on his black overcoat. He said goodbye to Joanna and Susan. He leaned down to me and kissed me. His cheek was scratchy, like sandpaper.

"Goodbye, Daddy. Get well soon, Daddy."

"Goodbye, Christine. Remember to pray for me. I love you."

"I love you, too."

After the front door closed behind them, I walked around the house, not sure which room to settle in. I couldn't sit on the living room couch. It was empty now, but it was still full of thoughts of Daddy's lean frame stretched the length of it. Soon it was time for bed.

After one week I wanted to visit Daddy in the hospital. I missed sitting on his lap. I had to see him.

"Please, Mother, couldn't I visit him just once? Can't

you talk to the doctor and get him to let me in?"

"Chrissie, Daddy is very sick. You would have to be very quiet."

Of course I would be quiet. Wasn't I the best behaved child in Mrs. Friday's class?

"When can I visit him, Mother?"

"I don't think it would be a good idea, Christine. You're too young to see someone so sick."

Too young to see my father? I knew the answer was no. But I tried anyway.

"Mother, couldn't I just stand at the window and look in, like I did last time he was in the hospital?"

The answer was no. Day by day went by and I didn't go to the hospital.

One Saturday morning I rattled around inside our house, unable to settle down and read the book I had brought home from the school library. I curled up in the little alcove beside the kitchen to eavesdrop on a conversation Mother was having with the pastor of our church.

Something about next Tuesday. Having part of the service in German. . . Orlando Harms would preach a sermon. . . I wasn't really listening.

After the pastor left, Mother found me meandering through the living room like a stray cat.

"Chrissie, I have to tell you something."

I knew it was something important. I sensed it was something about Daddy.

"Chrissie, Daddy died this morning. He died very early in the morning."

What strange knowledge to put in front of me. And yet it seemed familiar, as if I had expected it. I didn't know what to say or do.

"He died." My voice was small.

"He was at peace when he died."

Silence.

"Would you like to talk about it?"

"No."

What would I have said? Here was the truth. Now I had to accept it.

The quiet Saturday morning melted into a confusing, people-filled time. On my birthday, many relatives were in town for the funeral. Each one felt they had to get a present for their fatherless little niece. I half enjoyed the attention and half felt guilty for enjoying it.

On Tuesday, the day of the funeral, I didn't go to school. When I walked to the front of the church with Mother, I noticed my entire third grade class sitting in several well-behaved rows near the back of the sanctuary. I was surprised and pleased they had come.

"I could see Daddy today," I thought at the funeral. I thought the casket was probably open at the back of the church. But it wasn't the same, I decided. I didn't look, nor did I ask Mother if I could.

Sometimes after the funeral I was angry at my mother. Daddy had died, and I hadn't seen him. I wasn't satisfied with the goodbye I had given him. It wasn't honest. I hadn't known he wouldn't come back. I wanted another chance to see him while I knew he was dying. I blamed Mother because she hadn't taken me to the hospital when I wanted to go.

Gradually the brunt of my anger changed from Mother to something bigger. The "something" was composed of many things—the rules of the hospital that forbade seven-year-olds to visit their relatives; the doctors and nurses who refused to waive the rules; the power of grownups to have their way over me.

I was angry at these things, but mostly at the inescapable fact of Daddy's death. The lowering of the casket in the hole under the fir trees was so final and uncontrollable.

His death was too big a fact for me. I couldn't understand what it meant, and I couldn't change the fact. My anger became frustration. Piece by piece, I let the frustration slip from me to the hard November ground.

I write this in November, the same month my father died. I have lived in Hillsboro thirteen years. I have been a Christian thirteen years. My father has been dead thirteen years.

During my gradeschool years I didn't look at the negative results of Daddy's death. To people who tried to pity me I mentally asked, "Why are you feeling sorry for me?" After all, everything continued as it used to. Our family situation was a little different, but it wasn't painful, at least not for me. Now Mother instead of Father went to work in the morning and my sisters did the cooking instead of Mother.

Although the situation wasn't painful for me, it was frustrating and depressing for my mother. I should have helped her more than I did. Instead my self-centered attitude assumed that "Mother will take care of everything."

In high school I became aware that our family situation wasn't as normal as I'd thought. During one of my mother's infrequent low moments I heard her say, "I wish Daddy were here." She was crying. The statement shook my self-centered security to the core. The question, "Why did Daddy have to die?" stabbed me for the first time.

I needed a father, and I didn't have one. I felt unsure of myself around men and avoided them. I wondered if I would have known how to relate to men if I'd had a father.

My mother needed a husband. Mother went to school, taught English, wrote articles, cooked, sewed, cleaned house, and listened to the complaints of four children. Even with a husband, the amount of work she did would have been monumental, more than should be expected of one person. Yet Mother did it all.

Why, God, why?

The answers came slowly.

I compared my mother with the way she'd been before Daddy's death. Before, she had kept the kitchen well stocked with homemade buns and raisin bread. She attended women's sewing circle and made Christmas bundles for needy children. She helped Daddy with a youth magazine. She read books to my brother and me. She put Daddy before herself, keeping the house and family in order while he went to graduate school and taught in a Bible school.

After Daddy's death, her personality began a metamorphosis into something quite different from the ordinary wife and mother she had been. She was forced to assert herself in financial matters. When an opportunity came to start work at Tabor College, she made the break from the publishing house where she had been doing proofreading. The new job demanded more responsibility and more of her writing talents.

A few speaking engagements cropped up in women's groups and churches. I sat in the front row and smiled to myself at the thought of Mother giving a speech.

More and more religious periodicals included articles by Katie Funk Wiebe. Because she thought a lot about religious issues, our dinner table often was a discussion session over these issues. Mother and my two older sisters talked and argued while I sat quietly and listened.

So, although I didn't know why my father had died, I was thankful for the changes it had caused in my mother. I liked my new, articulate, assertive mother better than the old one. Comparing her with my friends' mothers, I thanked God again and again for giving me such a liberated model to follow. Because my mother thought that women had great worth and use in the church, I came to believe this, too. I learned to value my gifts in writing and studying as I saw mother exercise hers. I saw how easy it is to commit the sin of burying talents and I tried to avoid it.

As a result of my father's death, a new relationship developed between my mother and me. During my adolescent years I often had big questions on my mind: Is there really a God? How can I know God's will? Many nights during those years I would come to Mother's room before I went to bed. She would be reading in bed. I would lean against her doorframe and begin to voice a few of my doubts. We would talk and talk until I got tired of standing and would come sit beside her on the bed. We would talk until I felt some light on the subject. Finally mother would say, "It's time for bed." I would kiss her good night and make my way to my own room. Often before I got out of the door she would add, "There's a book on my shelf you might like to read. It might help you with your questions."

In the summers between my college years Mother wrote long, inspiring letters, helping me answer the questions that filled my mind as I compared Hillsboro with a big city. How could people actually live in such a hand-to-mouth existence? What would it be like to be a chambermaid for the rest of my life?

Mother became my friend, as well as my teacher and spiritual advisor. I don't think she would be all these things to me if my father hadn't died. So although I'm not thankful for my father's death, I'm thankful for the relationship it has made possible.

Our state of need after Daddy's death has given our family a chance to know those who helped us—the woman who did weekly laundry when mother was too busy, the man who brought a tractor tire to our backyard and filled it with sand for us to play in, and many others.

But the most amazing result of Daddy's death is what my mother has accomplished. Because Daddy died, she has fulfilled the dream to write she has had since she was my age. She has written many articles for church publications. And now she has written this book.

Bibliography

for Chapter Fourteen

Clementina Butler, *Pandita Ramabai Sarasvati: Her Life & Work* (New York: Fleming H. Revell, 1922)

Elsie Thomas Culver, *Women in the World of Religion* (Garden City, N.Y.: Doubleday & Company, Inc., 1967)

Edith Deen, *All of the Women of the Bible* (New York: Harper & Brothers Publishers, 1955)

_____*Family Living in the Bible* (New York: Harper & Row, 1963)

Myrtie L. Elmer, *Conversations with God: The Devotional Journals of Myrtie L. Elmer,* begun in her seventy-eighth year and continued until her death. Compiled and edited with an introduction by Raymond E. Gibson. (Grand Rapids, Mich.: Wm. B Eerdmans Publishing Company, 1962)

Phebe A. Hanaford, *Daughters of America* or *Women of the Century.* (Boston: B.B. Russell, 1883)

Georgia Harkness, *Women in Church and Society* (Nashville: Abingdon, 1972)

John Langdon-Davies, *A Short History of Women* (New York: The Literary Guild of America, 1927)

Mary S. Logan, *The Part Taken by Women in American History* (New York: Arno Press, 1972)

Julia O'Faolain and Lauro Martines, eds., *Not in God's Image.* (New York: Harper & Row, 1973)

Page Smith, *Daughters of the Promised Land–Women in American History* (Boston: Little, Brown and Company, 1970)

Charles Caldwell Ryrie, *The Place of Women in the Church* . (New York: The Macmillan Company, 1958)

E.F. Scott, *The Pastoral Epistles of The Moffatt Commentary* (New York: Harper and Brothers Publishers, n.d.)